Mathematical Theory
of Advanced Computing

Wolfgang W. Osterhage

Mathematical Theory
of Advanced Computing

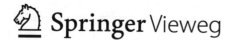 Springer Vieweg

Wolfgang W. Osterhage
Wachtberg-Niederbachem, Germany

ISBN 978-3-662-60361-1   ISBN 978-3-662-60359-8   (eBook)
https://doi.org/10.1007/978-3-662-60359-8

This Springer Vieweg imprint is published by the registered company Springer-Verlag GmbH, DE, part of Springer Nature.
The registered company address is: Heidelberger Platz 3, 14197 Berlin, Germany

Preface

This book is the English translation of Wolfgang W. Osterhage's *Mathematische Algorithmen und Computer-Performance*, Springer Vieweg, Heidelberg, 2016. It has been enhanced by the following items and sections:

- Chapter 5: Jump Transformations: Source code for computer art graphs and additional material in electronic form of 35 realizations of computer art
- Chapter 6: Data Management
- Chapter 7: Quantum Computers.

Initially this book originated from a collection of disparate papers all related to computer performance. Since a comprehensive work concerning performance had already been published (s. References), the challenge was to sort of compile a later supplement of these aspects and deliver it in an acceptable form. There are some special features in this book relating to two new algorithms and database theory, which have not yet been put to the test in the field. We hope to have called forth the interest of software and hardware architects alike.

On this occasion, I would like to express my special thanks to Martin Börger and Sophia Leonhard and their team for their patient support for this project.

Wachtberg-Niederbachem, Germany

Wolfgang W. Osterhage

Contents

Introduction

1

This book has to do with performance, but not as a general subject and not in completeness. It is about selected methods and how under certain conditions specific performance aspects can be improved. This means that—contrary to other publications (s. References at the end of the book)—for example considerations concerning process performance do not figure at all. The book is rather technical and partly speculative.

After an introductory chapter, which deals with the basics of computer performance and provides a general overview, there are six chapters dedicated each to specific algorithms and techniques, which may play a role under a performance point of view:

- Symbolic Execution (SE)
- Search-Based Automated Structural Testing (SBST)
- Preservation Numbers as an Instrument of Soft Computing
- Jump Transformations
- Data Management
- Quantum Computers.

SE and SBST are established methods in automatic testing of complex software. They are relevant to ensure and optimize performance during extensive tests. The concept of Preservation Numbers constitutes a new approach in soft computing and could be used in complex mathematical applications, for example for numerical modeling or simulations in the technical-scientific area. Jump Transformations present again a new algorithm, which may enable to generate overlapping numerical spaces on the basis of transformation boundaries, possible to be applied in the design of main memories to create competing address spaces within one and the same memory for example.

© Springer-Verlag GmbH Germany, part of Springer Nature 2020
W. W. Osterhage, *Mathematical Theory of Advanced Computing*,
https://doi.org/10.1007/978-3-662-60359-8_1

In the chapter about Data Management it is proposed to combine advanced data management techniques with artificial neural network technology.

Finally the concept of quantum computers and first realization attempts are introduced against the backdrop of an intelligence definition culminating in the speculation, whether quantum systems as such carry intelligence at all.

1.1   Terminology

The subject of performance optimization can be divided into three main parts of consideration:

- system performance
- application performance and
- process performance.

All three areas are subject to:

- theory
- measurement
- analysis and
- optimization.

1.2   Three Levels

When talking about performance people usually refer to system performance only— or to simplify it yet again: to the power of hardware, i.e. processor and main memory. This is the reason, why performance has been neglected during the last decades. At some stage hardware became so cheap that optimizing by programming techniques for example did not seem worthwhile, since manpower became more and more expensive. Hardware was bought and its extensions and as a result systems were running faster again. Or existing systems were configured so comfortably that performance problems just did not happen.

However, end user experience spoke a different language. Negative perceptions of response times did not only play a psychological role but also affected throughput in daily business. However, the ratio between hardware investments to optimization remained more or less constant over time. The reason for this is that generous hardware resources are exploited equally generously.

Only 50 years ago no one could afford memory allocations for blanks or binary zeros. Already at the variable declaration level and successively at the address level every single byte had to be considered deliberately. Otherwise major applications would never have taken off the ground. And finally, after the introduction of graphical user interfaces, C++ and Java and their derivatives structured programming in the classically sense was abandoned. Demands on ease of use, end user queries etc. played their part to resurrect old bottlenecks in new garments. In this way the performance debate has become newsworthy again—and this time not only restricted to systems and hardware alone. Although according to Fig. 1.1 the three levels

- system performance
- application performance
- process performance

are addressed one by one, the terminology in use initially refers to system and application performance only.

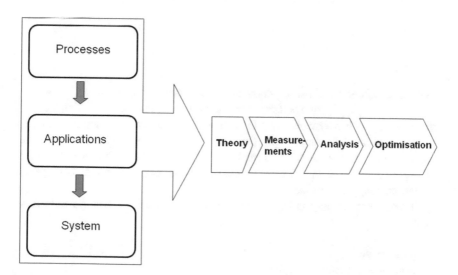

Fig. 1.1 Performance dimensions

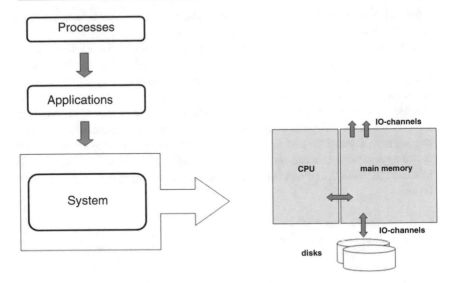

Fig. 1.2 System performance elements

System performance includes (Fig. 1.2)

- hardware utilization (memory, processor)
- configuration of system tables
- I/Os

with all procedures and parameters relevant to system management.

Concerning application performance and its analysis one has to take into account the interplay with system resources in detail, considering system resource calls, data management and I/Os for example. Quite generally speaking, if you want to execute applications you need systems to run them. Figure 1.3 shows the overall context. Thus, in performance considerations these two levels cannot be regarded as separate or just existing side by side.

Those elements playing the most important roles when analyzing applications are:

- program structure
- data management philosophy
- GUIs

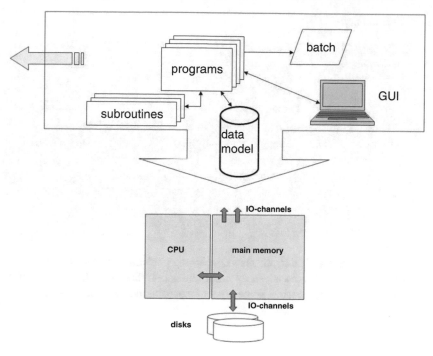

Fig. 1.3 Interplay between applications and system

At the top process performance dictates the rest. Process performance does not refer to system processors, but to those business processes, which are supposed to be supported by appropriate applications in turn running on their respective systems. This means that in our context those processes are not subject to the usual management consulting tools such as balanced scorecard, cycle time etc. The importance aspects with respect to overall IT performance are grounded in the consideration that in conjunction with a general optimization effort, the necessity of certain processes and their required system support demanding more or less resources can be put into question:

- Which system support is really necessary?
- How is my throughput influenced by application performance?

On this basis one has to decide eventually where to start with tuning first. This is the time when the cost-benefit question becomes really important.

In summary:

Performance problems are first realized at the process level when daily business suffers. At neuralgic points critical applications are identified. These in turn depend on the system on which they are running.

On the other hand, however, performance measurements begin at the system level and identify bottlenecks, which in turn relate to resource utilization by applications. Application analysis in the end challenges certain sub-processes.

The overall tuning package eventually includes a mix of measures at all three levels. Their prioritization for implementation depends on the expected economical benefit in an organization with respect to the costs necessary to do this.

These are the classical approaches concerning performance as such. Later in the book we will present more advanced possibilities to influence performance. Before this it is necessary to consider some aspects regarding performance theory.

Performance Theory

2

Here and in the subsequent chapters as well we shall deal with systems and applications separately. In practise, however, both aspects are intertwined with each other, and changes in parameters on one level will with near certainty have impact on the other. But there are at least two reasons for reducing the overall problems by separate considerations:

- Separate problem zones often are related to separate key challenges.
- Measures to solve problems can be specific to one level or another (without losing sight of possible interactions between the two).

A general picture of performance complexities usually presents a problem mix und thus aggravates singling out of critical aspects individually. In this chapter, therefore, we shall look at the two levels—systems and applications—one after the other. Because of their distinct nature the respective sections are structured differently.

2.1 System Performance

This section concerning system performance is again subdivided into

- hardware parameters
- operating system parameters.

Again those are in turn intertwined, since both depend on each other. Both aspects constitute what is called system architecture, and will in turn again be treated separately, where possible. The selection of operating system parameters

© Springer-Verlag GmbH Germany, part of Springer Nature 2020
W. W. Osterhage, *Mathematical Theory of Advanced Computing*,
https://doi.org/10.1007/978-3-662-60359-8_2

available obviously depends on the hardware manufacturer. On the one hand there exist a nearly infinite combination of operating adjustments with respect to a given hardware configuration of the same manufacturer—only constrained by the real existence of the applications to be supported. This brings us back to the already mentioned boundary conditions. On the other hand the same version of an operating system can be deployed on different hardware configurations.

Let's look at the hardware first.

2.1.1   Hardware Parameters

2.1.1.1 General Remarks

In actual fact this caption should really read: system or hardware components. The overall system configuration in turn can be subdivided into (Fig. 2.1 as Fig. 1.2):

- CPU
- main memory
- disk storage
- I/O channels.

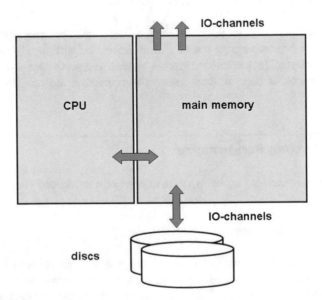

Fig. 2.1 System performance

Of course there are many more other elements belonging to the hardware domain, such as terminals, modems and communication components. They will not be treated separately here within the context of our performance considerations (such as configuring the cursor speed by mouse programs). The theory of system performance deals with those four elements mentioned above in this sequence. The importance of each component with respect to a specific performance situation depends on the type of application, the number of users and other factors. Therefore no priorities should be discussed at this stage.

These four components have mutual influence on each other. This will be explained in the course of the further discussions. Although the resources mentioned will initially be treated in isolation, their impact with regard to a specific performance scenario depends—as already mentioned—on the applications themselves, which rely on these resources. To isolate a specific problem one needs certain evidence to bring basic mechanisms into the open, which have influence on a specific performance scenario with respect to the application in question.

Before attending to the resources and their specific features in detail, some general principles should be addressed. The following questions are part of the discussion:

- In which way can system performance be tested generally?
- When does measuring performance make sense?

Performance testing is a discipline, by which in the end influence can be exerted over people, processes and technology to avoid risks, which can arise when introducing new systems, upgrades or patch installations. In short: performance tests consist in creating a typical system load before installing new applications—to measure performance, analyze it and collect end user experience. The aim is thus to identify performance problems under production-like conditions and eliminate them beforehand. A well prepared performance test should be able to answer the following questions:

- Are response times satisfactory for end users?
- Can the application cope with the anticipated system load?
- Is the application capable to accommodate the number of transactions expected from the business cases?
- Will an application remain stable under expected or even unexpected load scenarios?
- Will end users have a positive surprise, when the system goes life, or rather not?

By answering these questions performance testing helps to control the impact of changes and risks when introducing systems. In this sense performance tests should comprise the following activities:

- emulation of dozens, hundreds or even thousands of end users, who interact with the system
- consistent repetitions of load sequences
- measuring response times
- measuring system components under load
- analysis and final report.

Tests and analysis should take place before bottleneck situations occur (Fig. 2.2). Otherwise performance measurements would have to take place later on a running system, including later all relevant measures resulting from the analysis of performance data. This means that for example load distribution over a working day has to be estimated prior to applications going life. The same is true for the decision, which jobs to be launched at what times. Once throughput problems really occur after system introduction, the following sequence of actions makes sense:

- initially measure CPU under load,
- thereafter memory usage.

If CPU and memory show no problems, I/Os to disks should be investigated.

Besides pre-emptive performance measurements discussed so far measurements on production systems should be executed at regular intervals and

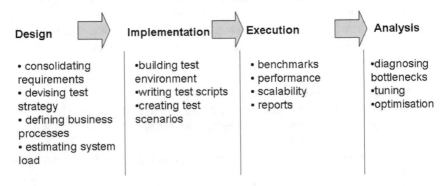

Fig. 2.2 Step by step approach for performance optimization (HP Document 4AA1-4227ENW)

continuously—especially then, when subjective suspicion about bad performance is reported: long response times for dialog applications, standard reports needing long execution times.

One problem, however, is the selection of a suitable yardstick. The subjective sentiment of a user sitting in front of a mute screen waiting for the return of his cursor—thus experiencing a pure response time problem—is normally not sufficient to pass for the status of a measured quantity. Generally one would want to examine—besides online functions or GUIs—additional batch runs, the execution times of which can be quantified, to get the overall picture.

Performance tests thus present a tool, with which to find out, whether a system update will lead to improvement or degradation. The conceptual design of such tests in the preparation phase should not be underestimated. It depends on the actual situation on site:

* number of users
* expected throughput
* existing hardware etc.

In any case it is important not to test isolated applications, but to either look at simulated real conditions or systems as they are found, comprising a significant number of system processes running in parallel.

Concerning individual users performance tests can be reduced to tangible key indicators:

* response times and
* dwell time.

These quantities have direct impact on work progress and thus on personal productivity supported by a suitable IT infrastructure. Business process steps accumulate purely operational time and waiting time for system responses or time for system non-availability. Waiting times are a direct consequence of the actual system utilization in each process step. In this sense performance tuning has a direct effect on productivity.

Against these demands stand the expectations of operations, emphasizing a different direction. Its interest is orientated on maximizing throughput on the job level. This means in reality high processor capacity utilization. Both expectations—those of the end user and those of operations—have to be taken into consideration to arrive at tuning compromises. For this certain bench marks are available which can be used as a case by case reference. These include not only technical data, but also estimates, which should help to avoid inefficient usage of system resources. Before taking first measures following a performance analysis the following clarifications should be made:

- Is the general emphasis on throughput only?
- Is the performance of the overall system unsatisfactory?

Quantitatively these questions could be narrowed down to:

- transaction rates depending on response times
- throughput rates depending on job execution times.

With respect to the user there are the following key indicators:

- response times belonging to different transaction types
- execution times for specific jobs that have been launched.

The performance of a complete system can again be traced to its various components; but also bad production scheduling can be the real reason, when job control is unbalanced. When deploying measuring tools one has to take into account that they themselves will use up some resources.

An important key indicator when measuring is the so called system time. It is the sum of the following items:

- controlling time sharing between several parallel processes
- controlling I/Os
- controlling swapping for main memory usage.

Experience shows the following benchmarks for a typical CPU:

- overall system time: 10–20%
- timesharing: 5–10%
- I/Os: 2–6%
- swapping: 1–2%.

Figures 2.3 and 2.4 give an indication of the essential approach and sequences of a tuning process.

At the end of these introductory remarks here are two more general observations: upgrading existing hardware is often not the panacea for performance bottlenecks, as will be shown further on. And: performance problems grow exponentially with

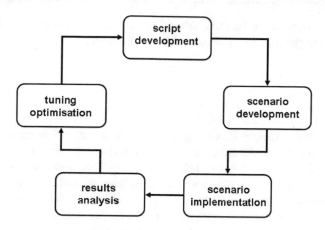

Fig. 2.3 Optimization cycle (HP Document 4AA1-5197ENW)

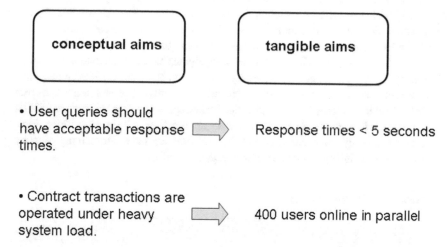

Fig. 2.4 From concept to objectives

the data volume to be handled. After these basic considerations the individual resources in question will now be examined separately.

2.1.2 CPU

CPU stands for Central Processing Unit. In the context of performance, CPU investigations focus on power, i.e. throughput through the processor. This power is measured in mips: million instructions per second. This, however, stands on paper only, which tells us something about the useable power and about overheads and task management without I/Os or wait queue management for other resources not being available or virtual memory management for that matter.

CPU power is a critical factor for those applications, which are strongly CPU bound, such as scientific and technical applications with long sequences of mathematical calculations.

One possible yardstick can be the "relative performance factor" (RPF) (s. Table 2.1). This quantity gives some information about the power potential of a CPU with respect to production conditions as realistically as possible. For its determination both online applications and batch processing are taken into account. For online the transaction rate is taken as a measure, for the latter the number of jobs executed per unit time. These measures are weighted in accordance to their relative importance in a given application setting: 20% batch, 80% online for example. But a single number alone is not capable to provide a definitive assessment about overall CPU behaviour. Normally the application landscape is too complex for that. Other factors of influence are given by the server architecture. All these considerations, however, do only make sense, when CPU performance and main memory capacity stand within some reasonable relationship to each other.

Table 2.1 RPF determination

CPU	RPF batch	RPF online	RPF weighted

A CPU can be in the following states:

- user busy
- overhead management
- waiting
- idle.

"User busy" refers to the execution of application tasks; "overhead manage-ment" indicates that the CPU is busy with managing itself, while going through waiting queues or redistributing priorities for example. "Waiting" points to the fact that a required resource is not available, and "idle" means that there are no demands on the CPU at present. Overheads can be broken down as follows:

- memory management/paging
- process interrupt control
- cache management.

These problems look entirely different in a multi processor environment (Table 2.2). This environment is constituted from central processing units on the one hand and I/O processors on the other. To optimally exploit such a configuration applications have to be written accordingly. This includes allowing for parallel processing without mutual interferences.

Such configurations have to be distinguished from others, which utilize parallel processors for resilience purposes to guarantee continuous availability of systems (Fig. 2.5).

On the task level a specific task can only be assigned to one particular processor and vice versa. This means of course that upgrading hardware by adding more processors has a limited impact to solve performance problems concerning response

Table 2.2 Increase in management overheads in a multiple CPU environment

No. of CPUs	Increase in CPU time
2	5–10%
4	10–15%
6	15–20%
8	20–30%
10	25–35%
12	30–40%
15	35–45%

Siemens: BS2000/OSD Performance-Handbuch Nov. 2009

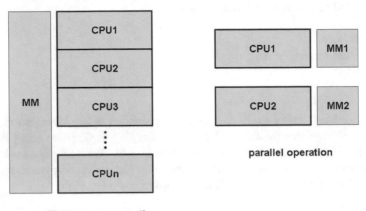

multi-processor operation

Fig. 2.5 Possible multi-CPU configurations

times. In the limit only a quicker CPU assignment takes place without any other throughput improvement. At the same time a significant acceleration of batch jobs can only be achieved by massive parallelism. Besides, one has to take care that by increasing the number of processors demand on synchronization with main memory increases as well producing additional overheads. Table 2.3 shows as an example improvement potentials for the execution of independent tasks by adding more CPUs.

Such upgrades generally mean that memory and disk drives will have to be adjusted upwardly as well.

Many manufacturers recommend reference levels for optimal utilization of their CPUs. In the following we shall concern ourselves with mono processors only. For online oriented systems CPU utilization should not exceed 70% for main

Table 2.3 Improvement effect after adding CPUs

No. of CPUs	Factor
2	1.7–1.9
4	3.3–3.6
6	4.6–5.2
8	5.8–6.6
10	6.8–7.8
12	7.8–8.8
15	8.8–9.9

Siemens: BS2000/OSD Performance-Handbuch Nov. 2009

Table 2.4 Load as a function of the number of CPUs

Load	No. of CPUs
75%	2
80%	4
85%	6
90%	8

Siemens: BS2000/OSD Performance-Handbuch Nov. 2009

application modules. In excess of that value, management problems concerning waiting queues can occur with the consequence of longer wait times. Naturally, possible utilization figures exceed these reference levels for a multi processor environment (Table 2.4).

To control CPU tasks certain routines are employed, which manage and supervise. The following parameters are important for task management:

- activation
- initialization
- multi programming level
- priority
- multi programming level (MPL) per category
- resource utilization (CPU), main memory, paging activity
- system utilities (CPU time, number of I/Os)
- assignment of access rights for main memory usage
- assignment of CPU resources
- state "active, ready"
- de-initialization
- resource usage at waiting times
- state "active, not ready"
- expulsion.

Since a CPU is used by many tasks at the same time, utilization is an important criterion for waiting times. The average service time by the CPU is, however, small in comparison to input and output times. This means that response times are influenced mainly by I/O processes, especially when reading or writing on storage media. The 70% utilization is determined solely by those. On top if this some manufacturers permit manual priority allocations, such that tasks that had been allotted low priority initially can now jump waiting queues. 100% utilization is an ideal value, which will never be obtained in practice.

Priorities refer to access to CPU resources, I/Os are not taken into account by this. Normally priorities are assigned in such a way that online tasks get higher priority with respect to batches. System programs on the other hand have even higher priorities than all other online functions. Within program processing the system itself calculates priorities according to a particular algorithm, taking into account waiting queue positions, swap rate and other parameters. Allocation of an external fixed priority is possible, should, however, be handled with care, since this priority will not be adjusted dynamically thereafter and could lead to the expulsion of other processes. In this way a few users, which deploy large programs, can be assigned low priorities against many users having to attend to only small tasks. At short notice urgent business functions could be assigned higher priorities as well as memory intensive programs blocking everything else, to liberate the system.

When talking about high CPU utilization the figure is around 90%. This does not necessarily mean a bottleneck situation. At high utilization, however, it is important to watch the efficiency of CPU operations. The following measures should be observed:

- checking the level of the I/O rate
- checking the level of the paging rate.

One measure for the efficiency of a given CPU at high utilization is the ratio of waiting time against CPU/hardware service time.

When longer waiting times occur, this may be due to the following causes:

- non optimal adjustment of system parameters
- The overall CPU time requirements for all tasks are too high. An analysis of waiting queues could lead to the causes of this situation.

An important role concerning CPU management is played by the handling of interrupts. Obviously swapping means the interruption of executing code. By this a program or a part of a program is stopped, the code segment swapped out of main memory and the task is directed into a waiting queue, from where it will gain access to resources later according to its priority (normally: position in queue). Interrupts can have the following causes:

- priority triggered resource access by the operating system
- termination of a self contained part of a program
- technical error ("exception")
- a longer pause when addressing a program page

- I/Os
- lacking data
- status "idle" with time out.

But even at low CPU utilization levels performance problems can occur. These can have the following reasons:

- I/O conflicts
- high access rate to storage media by many users at the same time (central data files)
- paging rate too high
- bottlenecks due to server tasks
- inefficient parallel processing for certain programs
- CPU time for the execution of certain programs
- too many system calls
- system self management
- too many library routines
- too many I/O routines
- too many users in parallel
- multi processor management
- unfavourable CPU clock cycle per process
- processor deadlock
- sequence of machine instructions.

If performance problems continue to persist, even when CPU is "idle", these problems are to be looked for elsewhere. By upgrading the CPU nothing will be gained.

2.1.3   Main Memory

One significant characteristic of main memory can be found in its nominal size, i.e. the number of bytes available for central processing and its temporary storage for this purpose. The absolute size of main memory with respect to a performance scenario can be

- just right
- too big or
- too small.

This sounds trivial. But the following has to be taken into consideration: an oversized memory, often recommended to compensate for bottlenecks, can lead to secondary CPU problems, when processing power does not follow in step, or will expose the limits of I/O channels. The reason for this is the number of possible tasks, which can be loaded and will exceed the capabilities of these two other resources in such a way that waiting queues will be generated.

Of course an undersized main memory is the most obvious problem. Main memory has to deal with (Fig. 2.6)

- program segments
- data
- cache partitions and
- parts of the operating system.

Normally some part of main memory will constantly be occupied by some basic functions of the operating system: base memory as a fixed portion of the overall storage space, 10% for example. Other portions of the operating system will be loaded later, when the need arises. An important portion will be needed for user processes. This is the reason, why special care has to be taken, when updating the operating system with a new version, which may include additional functions. Reconfiguring has to take this into account.

Fig. 2.6 Main memory usage

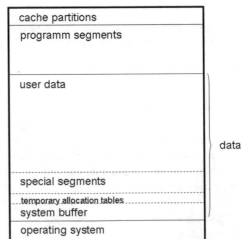

Cache partitions are needed for storage segments containing data, which are addressed repeatedly. These partitions can be configured but also be assigned dynamically. The latter does not present a particular problem for the cache, even when bottlenecks may lead to restrictions concerning the cache portion and part of it is outsourced to a disk. Performance then degrades by the fact that some cache data now have to be read directly from the disk. On the other hand intensive cache usage leads to interrupts and address mapping. This in turn generates additional CPU overheads.

Data occupancy of main memory has the following sources:

- user data
- temporary addressing tables
- special segments
- system buffers.

User data occupy the address space, which has been assigned to a specific user for sorts for example. Special segments are used for messaging or communication buffers and system buffers for certain system tasks. The rest is available for program segments or for paging.

An important factor when judging main memory performance is the paging rate. Paging rate is defined by the number of instances per unit time, when actual memory resident code pages being used for the execution of a program by the CPU are temporarily removed, replaced by others and the original pages later again be reloaded. This sequence is called swapping.

There are some algorithms identifying those main memory entries, which are earmarked for swapping. Normally the resource waiting queues are polled by each system cycle within the frequency of the system clock to find out which segments have not been addressed during the previous cycle. Those will be flagged as overlay candidates. During the next cycle the overlay candidates are again checked and possibly swapped, if memory space is needed. If there are many overlay candidates and long dwell times for certain segments, which could be swapped without process interruption, only marginal memory management overheads will occur.

High paging rates can be critical for an efficient use of the main memory resource (Fig. 2.7). Reasons for this are:

- too many processes
- programs with too large a size.

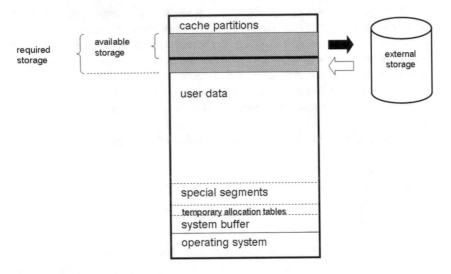

Fig. 2.7 Paging

Therefore manufacturers release recommended maximum values. Memory management for a smoothly performing CPU should not account for more than a few percentage points. Otherwise paging rates, which are too high, will lead to bad response times, because CPU resources will be used for that. Background: in both cases mentioned above the CPU first tries to reorganise main memory occupation by creating a concatenated address space (generating considerable overheads). If this does not work, the CPU gives up, i.e. processes of low priority will be interrupted, swapping takes place into virtual memory or into the paging areas on the disks. Consequences are:

• lost CPU resources for memory management (increase in subjective response times)
• interrupted user processes (increase in subjective response times).

In case these problems become chronical there is no way around an upgrade of main memory. One reason for this is that external swapping areas have to be specially configured. If they are too small paging becomes a secondary bottleneck with additional I/O waiting times and corresponding memory management.

To avoid main memory bottlenecks it makes sense to regularly and prophylactically take measurements with a suitable monitor. The following values should be captured:

- the number of pageable pages (size of main memory minus the number of pages in permanent residence necessary for system purposes)
- the number of globally used pages (number of pageable pages minus the number of freely usable pages).

Similarly to CPU there are reference values for main memory. Usage of up to 75% is supposed to be non critical. By usage of continuously more than 90% an upgrade is unavoidable. As is the case for CPUs there is a task management with more or less similar triggers via control functions for main memory management including a page administration algorithm:

- activation
- deactivation
- forced deactivation
- expulsion.

Summarizing, the following scenarios can happen:

Memory demand is higher than available. This creates a paging problem. This means that certain process sequences will be relocated temporarily onto decentralized storage media leading to noticeable performance degradation. Solutions can be gained either by hardware upgrades or application optimization. On the organisational level the number of users could theoretically be reduced, which is generally not regarded as being acceptable.

The opposite scenario is given, when sufficient memory is available. There is no third option between these two states. In this context a specific program does not have to be loaded completely for the execution of certain functions. Program pages are loaded in accordance with their address sequences one by one leading in turn to swap-ins and swap-outs—thus paging processes. In any case statistics show that most programs remain during 80% of their execution time within only 20% of their own code. Inactive processes are mainly caused by online applications—when users remain in front of their screens and do not enter anything, while the program itself remains open via the GUI. To optimize with respect to paging the following measures can be applied:

- usage of common subroutines by several programs at the same time
- code size optimization
- usage of common libraries
- memory configuration with respect to the estimated number of users.

2.1.4 Disks

There are some simple facts that explain, why absolute disk space influences system performance: should totally available disk space be occupied by a theoretical 100%, the system will grind to a halt. Files can no longer be created (even temporary or spool files) or even updated. But, of course, there are other problems, which will be noticed much earlier.

Every system coming close to 90% disk space occupation will indicate performance problems regarding response times as well as anything as a smoothly running production environment. For problem free operations one needs free storage space for

- backups
- end of the month results or
- data base reorganisation.

These are the reasons, why disk occupation should not exceed 75%.

Normally users and administrators have only limited influence on the physical localisation of files on external storage media (volumes). One has to keep in mind that one physical volume may contain several logical volumes. Volumes are addressed via an identification number. Access times depend on the type of access technology, management of storage space, but also on the fact, whether a configuration uses several computers at the same time. Other impairments can be created due to parallel disk mirroring, especially in connection with the RAID concept. RAID (Redundant Arrays of Independent Disks) functions the other way round by grouping several physical volumes under one logical one. In this way a corresponding data redundancy is created.

Manufacturers offer modules for device management with the following functionalities:

- monitoring of disk occupation
- reservation of disks
- configuration
- surveillance of access readiness
- partitioning to optimise access to logically connected tables.

For all those reasons it is important to identify and plan for storage locations prior to new installations, determine where which data should be placed and design an appropriate schema before effective initial loading.

Compromises need to be found between the objectives of throughput optimisation of an individual process against the overall throughput for the whole disk. To measure a single process a large test file is required. For the overall throughput of a single disk this is more difficult. Actually this can only be achieved by a simulation covering all processes. Thereafter measures can be taken respecting the different interests of applications. Another compromise concerns the optimal usage of the storage medium with respect to throughput. In this case one has to distinguish: large files having little storage efficiency should be placed on a single defined disk, many small files on others.

Another aspect concerns the fragmentation of information (Fig. 2.8). It is indeed not the case that all data records belonging to a specific table should reside concatenated on a particular storage medium—not even initially. Files and data records are fractionated or split and distributed according to an internal algorithm over a disk together with corresponding pointers referring to respective subsequent

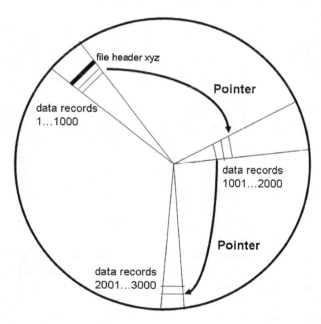

Fig. 2.8 Fragmentation of a hard disk

addresses. During the life cycle of an application this state of affairs degrades even more since files are updated by deletions or additions of data records. By this gaps on the storage medium are created; then these gaps are refilled. These new creations do not necessary belong to the same file nor are they in a specific logical sequence. In the end search processes for queries will be prolonged and thus response times. From time to time a defragmentation should be run. This results in gaps being filled up and associated data being brought closer to each other.

2.1.5 I/O

As already mentioned, there is a danger that a significant portion of CPU resources is required for the management of I/O waits. This is especially the case, when they are caused by process interruptions. Besides disks accesses themselves important roles are played by the number and speed of communication channels and their controllers. Those are also required for terminals, modems and other communication hardware. A too small a number of I/O controllers leads to communication bottlenecks. But on the other hand a given CPU can only manage a limited number of controllers itself.

There are strong dependencies between the performance of external disk drives and the capacity of communication channels. Some manufacturers provide control mechanisms as part of their data management systems for input/output processes. The reaction time for input/output commands is generally one order of magnitude longer than that for CPU commands.

To begin with our interest shall centre on input/output to and from external storage media (Fig. 2.9). In programs those calls are realised via intrinsics or I/O program calls (get, put etc.). SQL queries (read, write) are translated into equivalent execution instructions. Of importance for the execution of such or similar queries is the structure of the data bases in question. The duration of search operations differs for sequential files, index sequential files or relational data base management systems. Furthermore, execution times depend on the type of access. Reading access is obviously faster than updates, where a record has to be found first, then read and finally written to.

Once input/output is needed for the continuous execution of a program this part of the code is put into waiting until the input/output sequence is completed. Thereafter the program continues to run. From the point of view of the CPU the program rests in a waiting queue, which is controlled by a priority algorithm. This queue contains also parts of other competing programs, which means that the immediate execution of the program in question after the I/O is completed is not

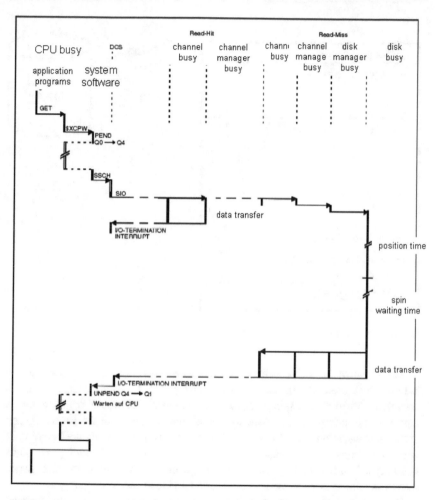

Fig. 2.9 Disk I/Os over time (Siemens BS 2000/OSD Performance-Handbuch Nov. 2009)

guaranteed, but will proceed only according to the actual internal priorities. In case the input/output happens via specific channels or special devices there are again waiting queues, since other users demand access to those resources as well.

Input/output is thus a complex process, which succeeds in combination with various waiting queues and data buffers, into which the requested data records are read.

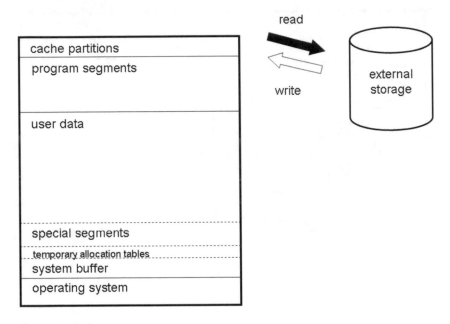

Fig. 2.10 Cache management

The so called data cache helps to accelerate accesses (Fig. 2.10). Data cache is a buffer, which stores those data requested last, while the user or the program is occupied with different things. Now, once the last request for some reason is repeated, this information is made available immediately from the cache. On top of this data cache provides for a minimisation of disk accesses and the bundling of write operations (write behind method). Data caches can be configured. Data throughput is influenced by their size. Compromises have to be found between cache reservation in main memory, I/Os and CPU load for swapping purposes.

I/O time depends in turn on the technology of the system bus and the channel structure for the I/Os. In case of several externals disks there have to be compromises between the total transfer rate across all disks and the individual transfer rate of a single disk. Maximising the overall transfer rate impedes the individual transfer rates. To optimise one can split applications in such a way that certain disks contain large files and others in turn many small files for less important I/O demands.

The optimum solution obviously is an even distribution of disk I/Os across all disks. Each disk should have its own controller. Shared controllers with several channels on the same bus should be avoided. To sum it up: transfer rates are thus depended on a combination of disks, bus performance and controllers. Optimisation, however, does not necessarily succeed by making all components faster, since new bottlenecks can arise by a good performance of one component to the detriment of one of the others.

Performance data of disks do in turn depend on the positioning time (time to move the disk head from one data track to the next) in dependence of data contiguity. In case of high fragmentation and data distribution across many applications, frequent jumps of the head will be the consequence. This in turn leads to accelerations and decelerations. For this scenario search operations themselves are much longer than reading or writing on their own. To improve this situation the various possibilities for partitioning provided by the manufacturer should be put into use.

2.1.6 Operating System Parameters

Every operating system carries besides its capabilities to support applications also its own proper functions, which influence and demand system resources. These comprise:

- program calls
- certain commands
- system control functions
- configuration parameters
- system tables
- functional subsystems: utilities.

Certain operating system commands can influence performance. Some of them are used for:

- communications control
- job limits
- logging
- memory allocation
- priority assignment.

Directly influencing performance are the following system control functions and configuration parameters:

- communication settings
- job limits
- logging
- memory allocation
- priority scheduling
- settings relevant for data systems
- spool parameters
- time outs
- cache sizes
- system tables.

System tables need special attention. Generally it is understood that table overflows will bring the system down. On the other hand, oversized tables will occupy too much main memory. Concerning utilities one has to decide on the organisational level which circumstances will allow to provide certain users or applications with which utilities. These utilities may include:

- editors
- system monitoring routines
- debugging software
- format handlers
- compilers
- data base handlers.

Besides all this it is important to check, whether new versions of operating systems contain features, which can positively be employed to improve performance. This should be an ongoing process.

2.2 Application Performance

2.2.1 Application Parameters

Although performance tuning on the basis of application parameters is usually time consuming and will normally not show visible results in the short run, it nevertheless is often without alternative to gain success in the medium and long term. These are some influencing factors:

- programming language
- program architecture
- number of subroutines and external calls
- data management
- I/O procedures
- GUI or batch processing
- size of code segments
- communication processes with other applications.

If it can be chosen the programming language plays an important role for the future performance of an application. This has to be put in relation to realisation times for a modular program architecture against the classical structured programs, which has lost in importance with the advent of modern programming languages. In a modular architecture application modules are decoupled from each other although united under a common front end. This relieves main memory. Besides, certain modules from different parts of an application can be addressed by different programs or other program parts and in this way be utilized in common—for example error routines.

Although one should expect that every new release will deliver acceptable application performance the results depend strongly on preparatory measures. They should take into account demands of the users and their performance expectations. The basic process sequences, which IT is going to support, has to be taken into account. In the end the following questions should be answered:

- Has the application architecture to be adapted to satisfy certain performance criteria?
- Will an upgrade of the IT infrastructure be required?
- Is performance degraded by GUI design?
- How will system load be affected by an expected increase of throughput?

Occasionally some factors can be tuned with small effort—like I/O procedures or a switch from GUI to batch. Others demand higher investments. The transposition from one programming language to another or changes to the data model belong to the latter.

In addition to measured quantities, which are of importance to system performance itself, there are a number of characteristics with direct relevance to applications. Task specific demands on resources over time and at peak hours belong to these. They relate to:

- CPU time
- I/O results including accesses to certain data tables and disk access statistics
- waiting times
- paging rate
- channel transports including TCP/IP connections
- possible communication events within a cluster configuration
- accesses to main memory
- response time statistics
- cache hit rate
- number of job executions.

This information can be gathered either by measuring monitors or partly from log files once the relevant transaction types have been flagged for recording. To record transactions log files need to be adapted specifically with respect to two criteria:

- formatting
- selection.

Formatting means, that care has to be taken, that entries are disburdened from technical information. This requires that everything with relevance to transaction codes or data encryption, format declarations etc. should be spared. Only readable text information should be deposited, which give an immediate indication to the analyst about what is happening with a particular transaction.

Only such transactions should be earmarked for recording that are of relevance to a later analysis. Negligible functions like "show date", "return to main menu" etc. should be suppressed.

Furthermore averages and peak recordings over time for a typical working day are of interest. These will show time dependent bottlenecks, which could initially be decoupled by organisational measures without major technical efforts. Concerning the number of users behind resource utilisation one has to differentiate between active ones and those, which are only logged in and remain idle otherwise.

Bibliography

1. W. Osterhage, *Computer Performance Optimization* (Springer, Heidelberg, 2012)

Test-Automatisation

3

3.1 Introduction

Performance plays an important role not only during production and operation of any application but also regarding extensions or introducing new applications and with respect to test operations. To design relevant test procedures with an acceptable data throughput as general as possible there are several algorithms on offer, of which we shall present two important ones in this chapter.

Initially we will introduce the motivation for automated testing. Then we will contrast the most important aspects of manual with automated testing.

There exist a number of automated test procedures. In part they are written by the development crews of major software houses with a view to serve their specific purposes. After basic considerations two procedures will be presented, which have established themselves worldwide in the developer community:

- Symbolic Execution (SE)
- Search-Based Automated Structural Testing (SBST)

For both of them a short summary of present day state-of-the-art will be given at the end [1].

3.2 Why Automatisation?

Usually there are two different approaches for extensive tests (Fig. 3.1)

- manual procedures
- automatisation.

© Springer-Verlag GmbH Germany, part of Springer Nature 2020
W. W. Osterhage, *Mathematical Theory of Advanced Computing*,
https://doi.org/10.1007/978-3-662-60359-8_3

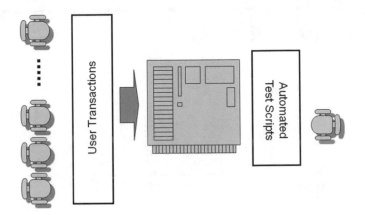

Fig. 3.1 Manual against automated testing

Unfortunately manual testing implies some disadvantages:

- difficulty to emulate the conduct of a large number of users
- efficient coordination of user operations
- comparison between different test scenarios is difficult.
- Also, manual testing is often not very practical. If one wants to diagnose a problem exactly, the same tests have to be repeated several times. Software has to be patched, and thereafter re-tests take place to find out, whether an error has been fixed.

For automated testing this is easier. Certain tools provide the possibility to save the relevant test scripts and their results. Additionally, human mistakes during the test phase can be avoided. Such tools provide the following components (Fig. 3.2):

- control unit supplying test input and controlling it
- virtual user landscape (User-Generator)
- automated test scripts for online simulation (they always have to be tailor-made with respect to the applications in question)
- monitor
- analysis machine.

This enables the following (Fig. 3.3):

- replacement of manual users by virtual ones
- simultaneous deployment of many virtual users on one and the same system
- repetition of scenarios to verify the effect of adjustments.

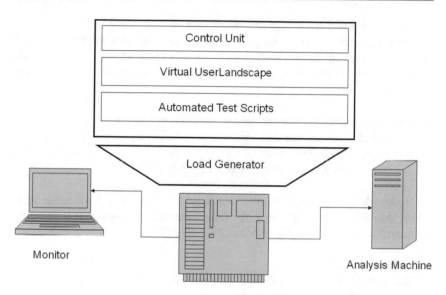

Fig. 3.2   Automated test-tool

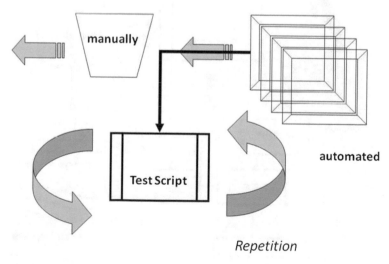

Fig. 3.3   Automated test possibilities

In this way costs and resources can be saved.

Even for mainly manual testing automated testing and measurements can serve to support manual processes. Sometimes this is necessary, when end user resources are not readily available. In this way the following information can be gained (Fig. 3.4):

- repeated test sequences under identical conditions
- end-to-end processes and their behaviour
- automated recording of results
- monitor reports for individual system components.

Although the effort for automated testing during the test phase itself is much lower than that for single tests by many users, automated testing means a significant preparation effort. This implies among others (Fig. 3.5):

- definition of test objectives
- documenting business processes or sub-processes
- selection of transactions to be tested
- determination of the number of concurrent users

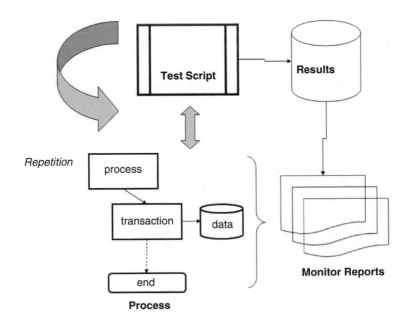

Fig. 3.4 Automated process tests

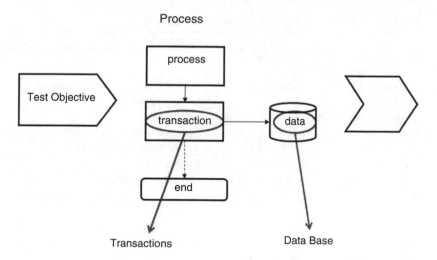

Fig. 3.5 Test preparation

- selection of data basis; for simulations: synthetic data or data from production dumps.

A further possibility for automatisation is the complete abandonment of real users. Instead scripts have to be written, which will complete the GUIs automatically with data and trigger transactions independently. To make sure that a process succeeds one has to provide for „data entry errors", and how the system should behave accordingly. During automated testing monitoring will show immediately where process problems happen. In this way all critical units can be polled and observed.

Another advantage of automatisation is the possibility to deploy such a monitoring for identical transaction sequences.

3.3   Comparison Between Manual and Automated Testing

Table 3.1 shows a comparison between automated and manual test procedures:

Table 3.1 Comparison between manual and automated testing

Function	Manual	Automated
To emulate a large number of users	Complex	Simple
Coordination of test operation	Necessary	Not necessary; control unit required; virtual user environment
Comparison of results	User dependent	Standardised
Test scripts	Process oriented	Process oriented; tool oriented
Traceability	Complex	Automatically by repetition
Evaluation	Complex	Per monitor
Error detection	By backwards searching	Immediate localisation

3.4   Symbolic Execution

One widely used method applied in automated testing is Symbolic Execution. With this method one can determine, which part of a program reacts to which kind of input. This is achieved by an interpreter. Instead of a specific input, which would be used in normal operations, symbolic values are used representing the complete range of values a variable can adopt.

With the help of these symbolic values results and variables are generated as well as conditions identified with respect to possible results for each branching within a program. Thus the output of the code depends on these values. To execute a code symbolically all input variables have to be initialized by symbols.

The objective of symbolic execution is to generate a test input for each program thread and in this way to finally cover the complete code.

A simple example for the test of a logical branching is shown in Fig. 3.6

The tool used for symbolic execution consists of two components (Fig. 3.7):

- program analyzer and
- constraint solver

The program analyzer executes the program while the constraint solver determines, which specific input variables are permitted. In this case the aim is to determine the value for a symbolic input variable, which makes the program terminate itself (constraint).

Instead of a numerical input the symbol "Z" is employed by the program analyzer. In the following command we receive as an intermediate result "3Z".

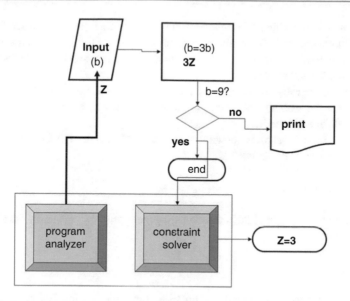

Fig. 3.6   Example SE

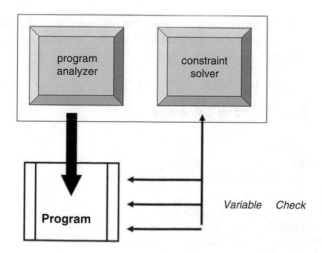

Fig. 3.7   SE tool

Thereafter a branching takes place depending on the calculated result from the preceding command. The analyzer then determines that the program ends itself for value b = 9 otherwise prints b. From this the constraint solver concludes that the program aborts for $Z = 3$.

Thus SE investigates, whether a code can be satisfied and if, by which values. Or vice versa: for which values it cannot be. Additionally an error check is performed for the different threads.

On the other hand SE is not without problems. There are a number of restrictions, which have to be observed:

- large programs:

The number of possible threads in a program grows exponentially with the size of the code.

- loops:

For certain loops the number of possible threads grows into infinity.

- economic viability

When certain threads are used by only a few different input values the employment of SE makes no sense and classical testing with a limited number of variables is more economical.

3.4.1   Challenges and Solutions

- thread explosion
    solution:
    - heuristic approach: arbitrary thread selection
    - thread prioritizing
    - parallel execution of program parts
    - combining the symbolic approach with specific data
- constraint solver limits: This can be caused by:
    - non-linear functions
    - library calls
    - indeterminable conditions

solution:
- exclusion of irrelevant side threads, when these do not influence the result for the actual thread.
- step-by-step approach using already existing results from previous steps
- iterative or approximative approach

- Data dependency: the execution of certain program loops can depend on specific data input to prevent the loop from executing indefinitely.
- PTOP: program-to-program-communication
    solution:
    - In this case the participating programs have to be tested in parallel, if for example the result of one of them serves as input to the other.
- external program calls
    solution:
    - They have to be treated just as library calls or PTOP.
- arithmetic operations: for them SE is generally of limited use.

3.4.2 Tools

In Table 3.2 there are some open source links for SE tools. Some of them are language dependent or may require certain processor characteristics.

Table 3.2 SE tools

http://klee.github.io/
http://babelfish.arc.nasa.gov/trac/jpf
https://github.com/osl/jcute
https://github.com/ksen007/janala2
http://www.key-project.org/
http://dslab.epfl.ch/proj/s2e
https://github.com/codelion/pathgrind
https://bitbucket.org/khooyp/otter/overview
https://github.com/SRA-SiliconValley/jalangi
http://www.cs.ubc.ca/labs/isd/Projects/Kite/
https://github.com/feliam/pysymemu/
https://github.com/JonathanSalwan/Triton

3.5   Search-Based Automated Structural Testing

SBST (Search Based Software Testing) applies optimization methods for testing such complex software, for which a wide field and massive combinatorics with regard to test data is conceivable. For this a number of algorithms are employed, of which the so called genetic algorithm is most widely used. This method had been introduced for the first time in the 70s of the last century.

3.5.1   Genetic Algorithm

Genetic algorithms are derived from evolutionary theory. Basically they are optimization procedures. The overall data space of possible input data is checked to find the best possible set (Fig. 3.8).

The most important elements of a genetic algorithm are:

- solution candidates: first generation
- fitness function: evaluation of solution candidates

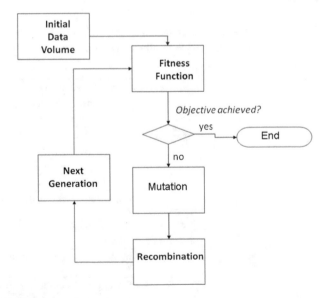

Fig. 3.8 Evolutionary algorithm

- heredity: next generation
- mutation: arbitrary modification of descendent
- recombination: combination of certain candidates.

To start off a set of arbitrarily selected inputs is chosen. From this the algorithm generates a new generation of input data by using mutations etc. Finally a fitness function decides about the optimal first generation of test data, i.e. those most suited for the test objective. In the end it is all about the optimization of data quality.

3.5.2 Limits

- impossible input

These may be test cases, which never turn up in real life.

- search extensions

The danger with evolutionary algorithms is the creation of more and more new generations, if no limits are employed (abortion criteria). This limitation, however, can be set arbitrarily and not with respect to any optimum, decided by a fitness function.

- Parameterisation

The algorithm has to be parameterized (for example: size of the input set, mutation rate etc.). The parameterization influences the optimization.

- local optima

It can happen that the search algorithm identifies a local optimum prematurely anywhere in software and thus stops. But this optimum may not necessarily be the global one, and thus the result is misleading.

- environmental problems

Any code is not a closed object, but interacts with a data base, with users, within a network etc. The whole environment of course influences the behavior of a program as well. The results of evolutionary algorithms have to be viewed in this context.

3.6   Combination of SE and SBST

We have seen that SE as well as SBST have certain advantages but at the same time limitations. The question is: can both approaches be combined to arrive in this way at better and more efficient test results? The problem is that both procedures have a completely different theoretical basis. In most cases the test problem is analyzed and then a decision taken about which method to be used.

In spite if this in recent years there have been efforts to compensate the weaknesses of one approach by the strength of the other. To achieve this different ways have been tried. To start with in general quite a number of parameters have to be investigated:

• What does technical integration look like?
• When will which method be applied?
• How many resources can be attached to each method?

At this stage two lines of attack shall be mentioned to address this problem:

1. Using existing genetic algorithms in series with SE. In this case the SE tool will find conditions for the results of SBST.
2. Employment of SE as mutation operator. On the other hand vice versa the fitness function can be used as a yard stick for an SE process.

There are some tools, which have specialized in the combination of both methods. Among them are:

• Evacon
• CORAL
• PEX
• Evosuite.

3.7   Conclusion

Automated testing has some distinct advantages against manual testing. We have presented the philosophy of two of the more important methods (SE and SBST). Both support a number of programming languages. For the application of these methods also open source tools besides commercial ones are available. When analyzing specific test proposals, however, the afore mentioned restrictions have to be taken into account carefully, before a decision is taken with regard to a definite test strategy.

Bibliography

1. I. Papadhopulli, N. Frasheri, Today's challenges of symbolic execution and search based algorithms for automated structural testing. Open J. Commun. Softw. (2015)
2. W. Osterhage, Automatisierte Verfahren für Software-Testung, in *Windows-Kompendium* (WEKA Fachverlag, Kissing, 2015)

Preservation Numbers: A New Approach in Soft Computing

4

4.1 Introduction

In this chapter the initial claim is made that a mathematical result in terms of its usefulness to real life applications is both a function of the type of operation and the relative size of the input parameters. To illustrate the meaning of this assumption the concept of "preservation numbers" is introduced. Preservation numbers are useful to classify any numerical operation into three distinct categories—depending on the type of operation and the relative size of the numerical input.

The formulation of the preservation number theorem leads directly to the concept of arithmetical efficiency. Efficiency again pertains to the type of operation and input to it. There is an obvious connection to any accuracy desired in a single numerical operation or a whole sequence of it. Both efficiency and accuracy will be formalized and related to each other. From this the selection of preservation numbers is triggered. Some practical examples will be shown to illustrate the concept. And finally the theorem of preservation numbers is introduced as a new approach for the negation of "tertium non datur" in logic systems.

Arithmetic efficiency and the accuracy theorem as well as the negation of "tertium non datur" present potentials for the optimization of applications and systems: the first to accelerate the throughput of technical-scientific highly complex programs, the latter as a basis for fuzzy like logics when designing system architectures or chips.

© Springer-Verlag GmbH Germany, part of Springer Nature 2020
W. W. Osterhage, *Mathematical Theory of Advanced Computing*,
https://doi.org/10.1007/978-3-662-60359-8_4

4.2   Calculations and Observations

Classical mathematical calculus is conceived to render predictable, exact and unequivocal results based on the rules relevant in a particular axiomatic system. The outcome of an operation depends on the operation itself. However, with the onset of fuzzy logic this picture became somewhat blurred. Now the purpose of an operation itself was not so much to obtain an unambiguous result, but one that would later on be sufficiently useful in the description of some part of reality.

In physics we distinguish between theory and experiment, i.e. between calculated and observed results. Observation obviously has no place in mathematics—with perhaps the one single exception of statistics. But there is nothing, which could prevent us to investigate the effect of mathematical operations with respect to the numeric values it aims to influence. In this sense "observation" takes place neither of individual operations nor of individual values but of the combination of both.

Let Z be any mathematical operator (for example +, sin. ln etc.) and p any number, then the entity that interests us is [Zp]. Our observation follows the change of the original input value by the operation Z—its input "history". In this sense Z could be interpreted as an experiment, which is executed on a particular input quantity, and the calculated result would then be the output of this particular mathematical experiment having been executed. Because we assume that the input value carries information (its absolute value, its algebraic sign etc.), our observation tells us about what has been left over from this original information: has this information been preserved in any way, has it been modified only slightly or has it been lost completely?

This can be illustrated by the following example:

Imagine three numbers, one being very small (e.g. 10^{-10}) (n_-), one in the medium "range" (between 1 and 100) (n) and the third very large (e.g. 10^9) (n_+). In this thought experiment the order of magnitude spread should be relatively uniform, not to allow for a justification for an alternative two-group split into one single extreme number and two closely separated counterparts. In our example we will initially only look at addition (subtraction) and multiplication (division). This leads to six possible combinations each. We will assign a "0" to an operation, if no significant change can be observed; a "1" if a significant change appears within the same order of magnitude and a "2" for a complete change of order of magnitude. The combinations and their effects can be seen from Table 4.1.

The number not participating in an operation gets a "0" assigned. Table 4.2 shows the same for multiplication and division.

Table 4.1 Efficiency values for addition and subtraction

Combination	Efficiency value for		
	n_-	n	n_+
n_- +− n	2	0	0
n_- +− n_+	2	0	0
n_- +− n_-	1	0	0
n +− n	0	1	0
n +− n_+	0	2	0
n_+ +− n_+	0	0	1

Table 4.2 Efficiency values for multiplication and division

Combination	Efficiency value for		
	n_-	n	n_+
n_- x/ n	1	2	0
n_- x/ n_+	2	0	2
n_- x/ n_-	2	0	0
n x/ n	0	1	0
n x/ n_+	0	2	1
n_+ x/ n_+	0	0	2

4.3   The Economy of Calculations

There are many applications in science and technology, where the results cannot be achieved by an enchainment of analytical mathematical operations alone. In practise quite often not all required input data are available or the operations themselves demand disproportionately high computer power or there are simply no arithmetic solutions at all. This has led to the introduction of fuzzy functions [1] and fuzzy sets [2].

On the other hand a number of algorithms has been developed for numerical calculations to solve the problems mentioned by other means, for example by the initial value method, Taylor series and the Runge-Kutta method [3]. The challenge regarding the approaches for actual calculations is the optimization of the required calculation steps to find a compromise between exact results and the necessary computing power.

To return to the overview of the previous section: apparently there are some [Zp] which are more economic than others depending on the actual combination of Z with p. This leads to three questions with respect to practical numeric applications:

1. Does a possibility exist to make chains of calculations more economic by leaving out distinct steps in a calculation?
2. What would be a useful basis to attain this objective?
3. How could such a basis be formalized?

4.4   Preservation Numbers

To answer the questions posed at the end of the previous section we introduce a new term—"Preservation Number" with the possible values $\{0,1,2\}$. Such a preservation number P_i has a similar significance as quantum numbers in atomic or nuclear physics: it describes a state and not a calculated or observed value. But—as will be shown later on—the logic between them follows a very distinct arithmetic.

Fully in accord with categorization in the example in Sect. 4.2 the preservation number obtains the value "0" for an operation, which does not lead to a significant change, "1" for a change within the existing order of magnitude and "2", when the order of magnitudes changes completely.

A preservation number thus reveals something about a specific mathematical operation in connection with particular orders of magnitude and about the economy of a particular operation [Zp], about loss of information or changes during a calculation process.

4.5   Definitions

For our further discussions we shall define two terms, which will be useful for the formalization of Preservation Numbers: accuracy and efficiency.

4.5.1   Accuracy

The term "accuracy" is widely used in statistics [4–6] and is applied in technical and scientific measurements. In our context, however, we propose to apply it in a similar fashion to the results of mathematical calculations. One could also have used the term "precision". However the term "precision" would have been deceptive, since precision could determine a well defined range of values within narrow boundaries, but without all considered precise events being necessarily accurate at all [7].

▶ **Definition** *Accuracy* is an attribute for an output value, which describes the deviation Δp_c from the associated input value after a mathematical operation. The information content of a numerical entity can be regarded as accurate, if it corresponds to a given reference. The reference is derived from the mathematical or physical system under consideration. The accuracy value itself thus represents a measure for the deviation from the reference.

Let p_o be the numerical value in question and p_r the reference.
For p_o to be accurate the condition

$$|p_r - p_o| \leq \Delta p_c \tag{4.1}$$

must be fulfilled—in our context $p_r = p$.

The *accuracy* of an operation is determined by the way the operation preserves the information content of a numerical value or not.

▶ **Definition** An operation [pZq] is accurate, if it preserves the input value to this operation on the whole. It is less accurate, if the information is changed (same order of magnitude). It is completely inaccurate, if the information content is lost completely.

4.5.2 Efficiency

There exist several approaches to improve the efficiency of mathematical models and associated programming [8, 9]. But their objective is just to improve existing calculation methods and models themselves to arrive at higher throughput and better performance. The evaluation of the efficiency of an operation as such with respect to their arguments [Zp] has until now not been the subject of investigations.

▶ **Definition** The *efficiency* E is an attribute of a mathematical operation as a measure, which describes the preservation of the accuracy of the same operation relative to the input.

In terms of engineering E can be defined as:
E = output/input. E should be $0 < E < 1$ (Second Law of Thermodynamics).

The closer E is to 1 the higher is the efficiency of a system, i.e. the smaller is the difference between input and output. In our context the input is a numerical value and the output a numerical value after an operation [Zp]. Therefore E could indeed be >1 or even $\gg 1$. For our purposes the following definition of E is useful:

$$E = 1 - \frac{|p_o - p|}{p_o + p}, \qquad (4.2)$$

with p being input and p_o being output.

We have to accept that this definition—although it goes along with a technical definition of efficiency—does not really correspond to the clarity, which one would probably expect in connection with the impact an operation Z has on any number.

4.6   Relationships

The following relations between accuracy, efficiency and preservation numbers were created to construct a formal model regarding the categorization of different [Zp].

4.6.1   Accuracy and Efficiency

With Eqs. (4.1) and (4.2) we obtain:

$$E \leq 1 - \frac{\Delta p_c}{p_o + p} \qquad (4.3)$$

An operation preserves accuracies, when this condition is fulfilled; it is carried out with the efficiency E. The efficiency of an operation again is a measure for the accuracy of the same operation with respect to the preservation of the latter concerning a participating numerical value. This goes for all positive numbers.

For $p_o \leq 0$ and for all real numbers **R** the efficiency equation has to be extended to

$$E = 1 - \frac{||p_o| - |p||}{||p_o| + |p||} \qquad (4.4)$$

4.6.2 Accuracy, Efficiency and Preservation Numbers

To express our categorization by preservation numbers we propose the following:
For $p \cong p_o$
E = 1; *accuracy* is high
$\Delta p_{c,o} \cong 0$

$$P = 0 \qquad (4.5)$$

For $p \ll p_o$
E = 0; *accuracy* is low
$\Delta p_{c,o} \Rightarrow \infty$

$$P = 2 \qquad (4.6)$$

For $p \neq p_o < 10p$, but not fulfilling Eq. (4.1)
$1 < E < 0$; *accuracy* is medium
$0 < \Delta p_{c,o} < \infty$

$$P = 1 \qquad (4.7)$$

These definitions—especially for $P = 1$, are soft and could always be accommodated according to the type of application. Here is an alternative;
For $1 < E > 0.9$ and $\Delta p_{c,o} \leq 0.18p$

$$P = 0 \qquad (4.8)$$

For $0.5|p| < |p_o| < 5|p|$

$$P = 1 \qquad (4.9)$$

with $0.9 > E > 0.6$ and $0.18p \leq \Delta p_{c,o} \leq 0.5p$ and
$0.9 > E > 0.3$ and $0.18p \leq \Delta p_{c,o} \leq 4p$
For $|p_o| > |p|$;
With $0.6 > E > 0$ and $|p_o| < |p|$ and
$0.3 > E > 0$ and $|p_o| > |p|$

$$P = 2 \qquad (4.10)$$

This means in terms of our definitions: efficiency is a measure of the preservation of accuracy, i.e. of the information value of a numeric entity in an operation—not a measure of the power of the operation itself. In fact the more efficient an operation in itself becomes the less efficient it is in terms of preservation.

4.7   Examples

Table 4.8 in the Appendix to this chapter gives some examples concerning mathematical operations and their effects on the information value of numerical entities in conjunction with certain value ranges (the values have been obtained from tables of Bronstein et al. [10]). The intervals have been determined using the efficiency criteria from Eqs. (4.5) to (4.7).

4.8   Chains of Calculations

Up to now we have considered only a single operation Z. In large numerical applications a long succession of operations can take place. There are obviously relations between individual operations and their respective efficiencies, accuracies and preservation numbers regarding just these individual operations within that chain, but also regarding the consolidated efficiency, accuracy and preservation numbers with respect to the complete chain. There are some useful definitions, which can help in assessing the preservation of the information content of such operations.

Let i be the number of successive operations, then

$$E_m = \frac{\sum_i E_i}{i} \tag{4.11}$$

is the mean efficiency of the chain, where E_i is the respective individual efficiency of each single operation.

Let E_t be the overall or total efficiency of the chain after the completion of all operation then

$$E_t/E_m = T \tag{4.12}$$

is the *transparency* of the overall operation, i.e. the ratio between the total efficiency and the average efficiency.

$$E_i/E_m = E_r \tag{4.13}$$

is the *relative incremental efficiency* as the ration between the individual efficiency and the average efficiency.

$$E_i/E_t = E_f \tag{4.14}$$

is the *fractional efficiency* as the ratio between each individual efficiency and the total efficiency at the end of every calculation chain.

These definitions may be useful, when modelling large scale applications with the possibility of changing the sequence of operations. On the other hand it is possible to assign preservation numbers to the chain itself.

By taking into account operations with $P = 0$ – like simple additions of small numbers to a very large one, the operation itself can theoretically be neglected. However, if in a chain of operations in a loop of a computer program the number of additions in total becomes such that in the end the preservation number of the complete chain amounts to let us say $P - 1$ or even $P = 2$, the individual negligence argument no longer holds. Because two parallel processes have taken place:

– an individual successions of incremental steps until the final value is reached and
– a succession of jumps, whenever a trigger criterion has been reached to merit a transition from P_i to P_{i+1}.

If $E_i = $ const. $= 1$ and $P = 0$ initially and $p = p_o + n\Delta p$, where n is any number of calculation steps, then the efficiency at the jump point for $P_i \rightarrow P_{i+1}$, the "jump efficiency", is

$$E_j = 1 - \frac{||p_o| - |p_o + nj\Delta p||}{||p_o| + |p_o + nj\Delta p||} \tag{4.15}$$

with n_j the number of calculation steps executed.

The above considerations can be extended to series as well. One example would be the jump transformation presented in the following chapter.

4.9 Logic

Just as Fuzzy Theory has its own logic with respect to Boolean logic the theory of preservation numbers is founded on its own logic. Whereas Boolean logic clearly follows the principle "tertium non datur", i.e. it only permits two different states of truth (Tables 4.3 and 4.4), fuzzy logic breaks with that rule, because it allows for an infinite number of truths. Additionally there has been a number of approaches introducing three or more dedicated states of truth [11].

In our case we look at three possibilities of truth, as can be expected with three possible preservation numbers (Table 4.5). True and false obviously are represented

Table 4.3 Boolean logic (conjunction)

∧	0	1
0	0	0
1	0	1

Table 4.4 Boolean logic (disjunction)

∨	0	1
0	0	1
1	1	1

Table 4.5 Logical values

Preservation number	Logical value
0	True
1	True(2)/false(0)
2	False

Table 4.6 Logical operation ∧

∧	0	1	2
0	0	0	0
1	0	1	1
2	1	1	2

Table 4.7 Logical operation ∨

∨	0	1	2
0	0	1	2
1	1	1	2
2	2	2	2

by $P = 0$ and $P = 2$, whereas the meaning of $P = 1$ may differ. From this a preservation number arithmetic can be constructed (Tables 4.6 and 4.7).

4.10   Applications

The presented number theorem could be important in various applications. The most important of them is the optimization of programs covering highly intensive numerical calculations. By using calculation filters computer resources could be saved. By suitably tailoring applications and evaluating the calculation steps with the help of preservation numbers certain calculation chains could be left out (Fig. 4.1).

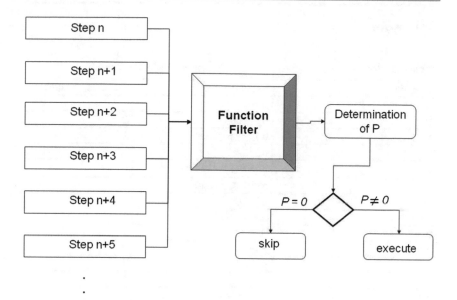

Fig. 4.1 Function filter

The function filter could be constructed as shown in Table 4.8 in the appendix. Other fields of applications could be:

- Data base access calculations
- Chip design using preservation number logic

Glossary

E   efficiency
E_f fractional efficiency
E_m mean efficiency
E_r relative incremental efficiency
p   any number
P_i preservation number
p_o output value
p_r reference value Δp_c accuracy
T   transparency
Z   any mathematical operator

Appendix

Table 4.8 Preservation numbers for certain vale ranges of different functions

Operation	Value range p	Preservation number P
$\log^{10}$	p > 1	2
ln	p > 100	2
e	$0.11 \leq p \leq 3.5$	1
	$p \geq 3.5$	2
$\sqrt[2]{}$	$0.995 \leq p \leq 1.004$	0
	$1.004 \leq p < 10$	1
	$p \geq 10$	2
sin	$0.52 < p < 1$	1
cos	$0.52 < P < 1.05$	1
arc	p = 0	0
	$p \neq 0$	2
tan	$0.52 < p < 1.05$	1
cot	$0.52 < p < 1.05$	1
arctan	$10 > p > 1$	1
	p > 10	2
arcsin	(except for $p \to 0$)	1
arccos		1
arcctg	$10 > p > 1$	1
	p > 10	2
sh	$4 > p > 1$	1
	p > 4	2
th	$1 < p < 10$	1
	p > 10	2
Γ	p = 1	0
	else	1
	$p \geq 1.6$	2
Bessel Functions J_0	$p \approx 0.8$	0
	$0.8 \geq p \geq 0.2$	1
	$2.0 \geq p \geq 0.8$	1
	$p \geq 2.0$	2
J_1		2
Y_0	$p \leq 0.2$	2
	$0.6 \geq p \geq 0.2$	1
	$p \geq 0.6$	2

(continued)

Table 4.8 (continued)

Operation	Value range p	Preservation number P
Y_1	$p \geq 0.35$	2
	$1.2 \geq p \geq 0.35$	1
	$p \geq 1.2$	2
I_0	$p \leq 0.2$	2
	$4.9 \geq p \geq 0.2$	1
	$p \geq 4.9$	2
I_1	$p \leq 0.4$	2
	$2.5 \geq p \geq 0.4$	1
	$p \approx 2.5$	0
	$5.0 \geq p \geq 2.5$	1
	$p \geq 5.0$	2
K_0	$p \leq 0.3$	2
	$0.9 \geq p \geq 0.3$	1
	$p > 0.9$	2
K_1	$p > 1.8$	2
	$0.8 \geq p \geq 1.5$	1
	$p \approx 0.8$	0
	$p \geq 1.5$	2
Legendre polynomials P_2	$p \leq 0.1$	2
	$0.3 \geq p \geq 0.1$	1
	$0.35 \geq p \geq 0.3$	0
	$0.5 \geq p \geq 0.35$	1
	$0.8 \geq p \geq 0.5$	2
	$0.99 \geq p \geq 0.8$	1
	$p \approx 1.0$	0
P_3	$p \leq 0.03$	2
	$0.3 \geq p \geq 0.03$	1
	$0.35 \geq p \geq 0.3$	0
	$0.4 \geq p \geq 0.35$	1
	$0.49 \geq p \geq 0.4$	0
	$0.7 \geq p \geq 0.49$	1
	$0.9 \geq p \geq 0.7$	2
	$0.99 \geq p \geq 0.9$	1
	$p \approx 1.0$	0
P_4	$p \leq 0.07$	2
	$0.2 \geq p \geq 0.07$	1
	$p \approx 0.2$	0

(continued)

Table 4.8 (continued)

Operation	Value range p	Preservation number P
	$0.24 \geq p \geq 0.2$	1
	$0.5 \geq p \geq 0.24$	2
	$0.8 \geq p \geq 0.5$	1
	$0.95 \geq p \geq 0.8$	2
	$0.99 \geq p \geq 0.95$	1
	$p \approx 1.0$	0
P_5	$p \leq 0.04$	2
	$0.3 \geq p \geq 0.04$	1
	$0.37 \geq p \geq 0.3$	0
	$0.43 \geq p \geq 0.37$	1
	$0.55 \geq p \geq 0.43$	2
	$0.75 \geq p \geq 0.55$	1
	$0.99 \geq p \geq 0.98$	2
	$p \approx 1.0$	0
P_6	$p \leq 0.06$	2
	$0.16 \geq p \geq 0.06$	1
	$p \approx 0.16$	0
	$0.19 \geq p \geq 0.16$	1
	$0.98 \geq p \geq 0.65$	2
	$0.999 \geq p \geq 0.98$	1
	$p \approx 1.0$	0
P_7	$p \leq 0.03$	2
	$0.26 \geq p \geq 0.03$	1
	$p \approx 0.26$	0
	$0.33 \geq p \geq 0.26$	1
	$0.52 \geq p \geq 0.33$	2
	$0.6 \geq p \geq 0.52$	1
	$0.99 \geq p \geq 0.6$	2
	$p \approx 1.0$	0
!	$2 \geq p \geq 1$	0
	$3 \geq p > 2$	1
	$p > 3$	2

References

1. A. Mayer et al., *Fuzzy Logic* (Addison-Wesley, 1993)
2. G.J. Klir, B. Yuan, *Fuzzy Sets and Fuzzy Logic* (1995)
3. J.C. Butcher, *The Numerical Analysis of Ordinary Differential Equations: Runge-Kutta and General Linear Methods* (1987)
4. E.W. Weisstein, *Accuracy*, from MathWorld – a Wolfram Web Resource, http://mathworld.com/Accuracy/html. Accessed 08 Aug 2019
5. S. Gililisco, N.H. Crowhurst, *Mastering Technical Mathematics* (McGraw-Hill Professional, 2007)
6. J.R. Taylor, *An Introduction of Error Analysis: The Study of Uncertainties in Physical Measurements* (Science Books, 1997), pp. 128–129
7. Clamson University, Physics Lab Tutorial, *Accuracy & Precision* (Department of Physics & Astronomy, South Carolina, 2000)
8. A. Schrijver, *Combinatorical optimization* (Springer, 2003)
9. I.K. Argyros, *Advances in the Efficiency of Computational Methods and Applications* (World Scientific Publishing, 2000)
10. I.N. Bronstein et al., *Taschenbuch der Mathematik* (Verlag Harri Deutsch, 2005)
11. L. Kreiser et al., *Nicht-klassische Logik* (Akademie-Verlag, Berlin, 1990)

Jump Transformations

5

5.1   Introduction

Ranges of numbers are known from mathematics and physics (Euler's Number Plane, Hilbert Space). Numbers are assigned symbols: 1 for "one", 15 for "fifteen". Symbols represent number values. One can distinguish between value ranges and symbol ranges. In our decimal system symbol and value ranges coincide. For the character or symbol ranges in computers matters are different:

Binary system with only two symbols 0 and 1:

$$\text{"five"} \to 101$$

Hexadecimal systems with 16 symbols:

$$\text{"twelve"} \to C$$

Such assignments are also called transformations. The term "transformation" is used to describe the change of a numerical presentation of a value from a decimal base to a non-decimal base—just like the conversion from the decimal system to the binary or hexadecimal. "Jump" transformations in this context relate to a trigger value, at which such a transformation within a certain number sequence happens. The transformations discussed here follow a sequence of base changes within one and the same type of transformation depending on rules given by the trigger value.

We shall first introduce the concept of jump transformation itself and then turn to a special type of transformation relating to a trigger based on n-tuple sequences of numbers. A set of rules is introduced for these particular transformations, although initially they may look to be arbitrary and could indeed be replaced by other similar ones. But as will be shown later, a modified approach though would lead to much the same consequences, when employed. The rules themselves lead to certain

© Springer-Verlag GmbH Germany, part of Springer Nature 2020
W. W. Osterhage, *Mathematical Theory of Advanced Computing*,
https://doi.org/10.1007/978-3-662-60359-8_5

characteristics of n-tuple trigger transformations, looking rather harmoniously in the first place, but can be explained logically. These transforms will then be properly formalised, and it will be seen that they follow circular algorithms. After discussing their graphical expressions, the possibilities of inter-relations between transformations with different n-tuple triggers will be investigated. These have some consequences regarding possible practical applications.

The n-tuple trigger will then be replaced by a random trigger. This leads to different transformations though with some of the characteristics remaining. Then the inter-transformations between any trigger transformations will be investigated. This is followed by further speculations about possible applications.

The application of most interest in this context could be found in improved architectures of main memory address spaces, containing overlapping non-interfering address fields, the addressing of which takes place via number ranges related to dedicated transformations. Additionally there are other possible fields of applications outside our original field of interest such as cryptography. These and other aspects will be touched upon briefly.

5.2   Jump Transformations

In this chapter "transformation" stands for the change of a numerical presentation of a value from one base to another—just like the conversion from the decimal system to the binary. As will be shown by starting out from a decimal basis a transformation to another base will be triggered once a specified condition is reached. Then a "jump" to another base will be executed. The conversion continues on this base until the next well defined condition is met, where upon the next jump to yet another base takes place and so on. Conditions and jump sequences are linked by pre-defined rules and can be calculated.

5.3   n-Tuple Transformations

The expression n-tuple describes the following type of number:

$N_n = a_n a_{n-1} a_{n-2} \ldots . a_1 a_0$, with $a_n = a_{n-1} = a_{n-2} = \ldots . a_1 = a_0$, the a_i being single digit out of 1 to 8 (the explanation, why 9 is left out, will become obvious later).

Examples: 444, 55, 7777, etc.

5.3.1 Definitions and Rules

Whenever for a given digit k between 1 and 8 an n-tuple configuration is reached, such that

$$N_k = k_n k_{n-1} k_{n-2} \ldots . k_1 k_o \text{ with } N_k \geq k_1 k_o = 11k \qquad (5.1)$$

a change of order of magnitude—a jump—takes place to a (decimal) base of the k_{n+1}th order of magnitude corresponding to $(k+1)^{n-2}(11k+1)$ (decimal) resp. 10^n (transformed).

Example:

Let k = 2. The following Table 5.1 registers, what happens:

A further definition is helpful for the discussions ahead:

(a) A jump is declared as major, whenever a jump is triggered by a change of order of magnitude ($22 \rightarrow 100$).

(b) A jump is declared as minor, whenever a jump is triggered within the remaining order of magnitude ($122 \rightarrow 200$).

Table 5.1 Example transformation

Decimal	Transformed
1	1
2	2
...	...
21	21
22	22
23	100
24	101
...	...
44	121
45	122
46	200
47	201
...	...
67	221
68	222
69	1000
70	1001
...	...

So, the first 22 numbers are based on decimal. After the first major jump the first digit is based on the base 23. This base holds until the transformed number 222 is reached, which triggers to 1000 with the base of the first digit being 69. And so on. The result is a number, where every digit is based on a different base, increasing with order of magnitude—except for the lowest two digits, which remain decimal based.

The above rule is restricted. The n-tuple condition is a closed one, i.e. it always applies forward from the last digit upwards. The case of an n-tuple sequence appearing somewhere in between the last and the first digit does not count as a criteria for a jump. There is indeed no logical reason, why such a transformation type should not exist. It is, however, not subject of investigation here.

5.3.2   Characteristics

The n-tuple jump transformations exhibit some interesting characteristics. Two laws can be derived:

1. If the base after the first jump of N_k is $11k+1$, then the successive bases are calculated as $(11k+1)(k+1)^n$, with $n = 1,\ldots,i$.

   An example for $k = 2$ is shown in Table 5.2.

2. Relationship between transformed order of magnitude and $(k+1)^n$:
   If a base is $(11k+1)(k+1)^n$, with $n = 1,\ldots,i$, then the corresponding transformed order of magnitude is 10^{n+2}.

   Example for $k = 2$: s. Table 5.2!
   The definitions, rules and characteristics cited so far are applicable to any $1 < k < 9$.

Table 5.2   Example of base calculation

Basis (decimal)	Transformed	n
23	100	0
69	1000	1
207	10,000	2
....		

5.3.3   Formalizations

Decimal lead:

$$l_d = 11k \tag{5.2}$$

Transformed lead:

$$l_t = 11k \tag{5.3}$$

Jump difference decimal:

$$S_k{}^d = (l_d + 1)(k + 1)^n \tag{5.4}$$

Jump difference transformed:

$$S_k{}^t = k \sum_{j=1}^{n+2} 10^j \tag{5.5}$$

Jump height transformed:

$$h_k{}^t(S_{k,n}) = 10^{n+1} \tag{5.6}$$

Minor jump difference:

$$d_{min} = 11k + 1 \tag{5.7}$$

Major jump difference:

$$d_{maj} = (11k + 1)\left[(k + 1)^{n+1} - (k + 1)^n\right] \tag{5.8}$$

Number of minor jumps between major jumps:

$$J_m = (k + 1)^{n+1} - (k + 1)^n \tag{5.9}$$

Jump condition:

Table 5.3 Nested process

	Decimal $N_d = 0$	Transformed $N_t = 0$
A	$N_d = N_d+1....l_d$	$N_t = N_t+1....l_t$
	$N_d = N_d+1$	$N_t = 100; J=1$
	$+1....l_d$	$+1....l_t$
	$+11k+1$	$+100; J = J+1<J_m;$
	....	....
	$N_d = (k+1)^{n+1}(11k+1)+1$	$N_d = S_k{}^t = k\sum_{j=1}^{n+2}10^j$
		resume at "A" until n

$$Z_j(k,n) + 1 = 10^{n+1}\,k \tag{5.10}$$

The total transformation follows a nested process. This can be seen in Table 5.3, with J being a counter.

Annotation: a function applied to itself is called a nested function [1], annotated as *nest*. Let

$$f_a = m\sum_n 10^n + 1 \quad \text{then} \quad \text{nest}_1\left[f_a, m\sum_n 10^n, l_t\right]$$

$$\text{and} \quad \text{nest}_2[\text{nest}_1, m, k] \tag{5.11}$$

$$\text{and} \quad \text{nest}_3[\text{nest}_2, i, n].$$

Let

$$f_d = N_d + 1 \quad \text{then} \quad \text{nest}_d[f_d, N_d, z] \tag{5.12}$$

The transformation can be formulated as:

$$\text{nest}_d[f_d, N_d, z] \Longleftrightarrow \text{nest}_3(z)[\text{nest}_2, i, n] \tag{5.13}$$

5.3.4 Examples

All transformations from $1 < k \leq 8$ have been calculated up to $N_d = 10^6$. Table 5.4 lists the key jump criteria up to the first three major jumps.

The graphs in Figs. 5.1, 5.2, 5.3 and 5.4 show $N_d \rightarrow N_t$ in sequence for $k = 1$, all $k = 1....8$, $k = 1...3$, $k = 6...8$.

Table 5.4 Jump criteria

k	n	l = 11k	d_{ma1}	h_1^t	d_{ma2}	h_2^t	d_{ma3}	h_3^t
1	2	11	12	100	24	1000	48	10,000
2	3	22	23	100	69	1000	207	10,000
3	4	33	34	100	136	1000	544	10,000
4	5	44	45	100	225	1000	1125	10,000
5	6	55	56	100	336	1000	2016	10,000
6	7	66	67	100	469	1000	3283	10,000
7	8	77	78	100	624	1000	4992	10,000
8	9	88	89	100	801	1000	7209	10,000

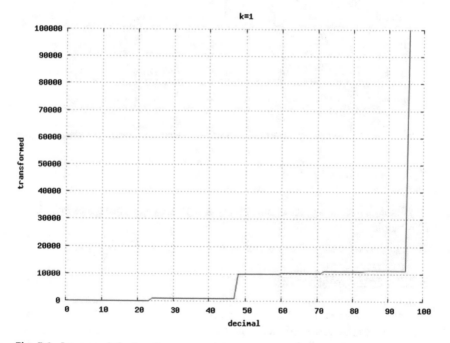

Fig. 5.1 Jump graph for k = 1

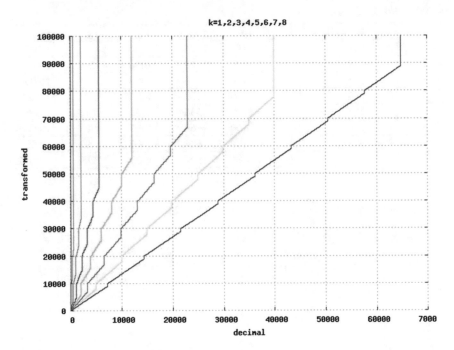

Fig. 5.2 Jump graphs for all k

Although lines do not make mathematical sense they have been chosen for better illustration.

5.3.5   Inter-relationships

Having transformed $N_d \rightarrow N_t$, the question arises, how a transformation from $N_{ki} \rightarrow N_{kj \neq i}$ can be described. Let us first consider the case of m < k. The transformation sought after will be $N_k \rightarrow N_m$. Until l_m both transformations are identical i.e. on a decimal base. Thereafter N_k continues on decimal until 11K, after which it switches in to its proper sequence. According to the transformation laws the sequence has to be checked against the next appearance of k-tuples. They will

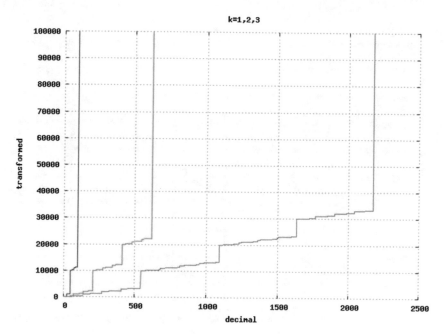

Fig. 5.3 Jump graphs for k = 1...3

never be found, since any m-tuple will always be smaller than any corresponding k-tuple.

The inverse case is $N_m \rightarrow N_k$. N_m switches into its proper sequencing after I_m. Thus the first condition of l_k will never be reached and a direct transformation is impossible. The deeper reason for this lies in the fact that transformations occur between numerical images and not values in the first place. An indirect transformation can however be achieved by an intermediate step using decimal values. The fact that inter-transformations cannot happen opens up possibilities for specific applications, which will be touched upon later.

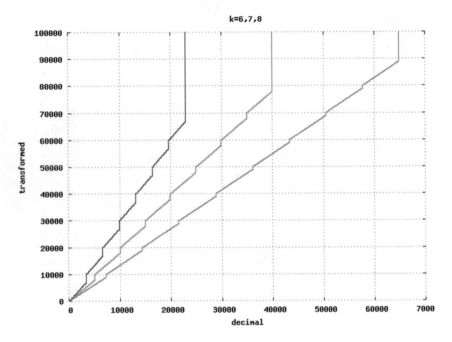

Fig. 5.4 Jump graphs for k = 6...8

5.4   Random Trigger Transformations

Up to now we have investigated jump transformations with n-tuple triggers. The next step will be to define as jump triggers any sequence of figures within a number like:

$$N_r = a_{rn}a_{rn-1}\ldots.a_{ri}\ldots.a_{r2}a_{r1}$$

with at least one of the $a_{ri} \neq a_{rj} \neq a_i$.

5.4.1   Definitions and Rules

Upon the first appearance of the trigger the jump is performed, like in:

Table 5.5 Jump conditions for random trigger transformations

Presentation	Decimal	Transformed
Number	$r_d = 10^n a_n + 10^{n-1} a_{n-1} \ldots + 10 a_1 + a_0 \leq l_r$	$r_t = 10^n a_n + 10^{n-1} a_{n-1} \ldots + 10 a_1 + a_0 \leq l_r$
Lead/minor jump differential	l_r	l_r
Major jump	$\Delta n, n+1 \rightarrow r_n a_n + \left(Mod\, \frac{r_n}{a_n 10^n} \right) + 1$	$a_n 10^{n+1} + 10 \left(Mod\, \frac{r_n}{a_n 10^n} \right) + 1$

$$N_d = a_n a_{n-1} a_{n-2} \ldots . \mathbf{a_{rn} a_{rn-1}} \ldots . \mathbf{a_{ri}} \ldots . \mathbf{a_{r2} a_{r1}}.$$

However, the very first time will be for $N_{df} = \mathbf{a_{rn} a_{rn-1} \ldots . a_{ri} \ldots . a_{r2} a_{r1}}$, transforming to $N_{tf} = 10^{n+1}$ in analogy to $l_{d,t}$ for n-tuples. It then follows a series of minor jumps with multiples of N_{tf} until the next major jump.

This condition is outlined in Table 5.5.

5.4.2 Example

Let $N_d = 51$. Table 5.6 shows the development of the transformation.

The graph in Fig. 5.5 shows the results. From a first impression the shapes looks similar to the n-tuple transformations.

5.5 Inter-transformations

5.5.1 Inter-relationships Between Two Random Triggers

Let N_{r1} and N_{r2} be two random triggers. The transformation goes from $N_{r1} \rightarrow N_{r2}$. Then the following rules apply:

for $N_{r1} < N_{r2}$: no transformation is possible;

Table 5.6 Transformation development for $N_d = 51$

Decimal	Transformed
1....51	1....51
52	100
152	200
+52	300
....	....
+52 (=5×52=260)	500
261	501
....	....
270	510
271	1000
....	....
540	1510
541	2000
....	....
1408	5100
1409	10,000

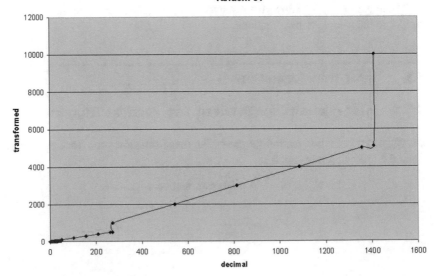

random 51

Fig. 5.5 Transformation for $N_d = 51$

for $N_{r1} > N_{r2}$:   let $N_{r1} = 10^n a_n + 10^{n-1} a_{n-1} \ldots + 10^i a_i + \ldots 10 a_1 + a_0$ and

$\qquad\qquad\qquad N_{r2} = 10^i b_i + 10^{i-1} b_{i-1} \ldots + 10 b_1 + b_0$

then a transformation $N_{r1} \rightarrow N_{r2}$ is only possible, if

$$10^i a_i + 10^{i-1} a_{i-1} + \ldots 10 a_1 + a_0 \leq 10^i b_i + 10^{i-1} b_{i-1} + \ldots 10 b_1 + b_0 \qquad (5.14)$$

5.5.2   Transformation Between n-Tuple and Random Triggers

The transformation $N_k \rightarrow N_r$ is possible under the following conditions:

$$N_k < N_r$$

and

$$a_{k0} < k.$$

A transformation $N_r \rightarrow N_k$ is not possible.

5.6   Applications

Although it is difficult to predict all possible practical implications of the above transformations, there are some tentative fields of interest that come to mind at this stage. Here, we will only touch upon these possibilities without developing into detailed technical solutions.

5.6.1   Sets and Address Spaces

In case of n-tuples let $K_{k=\{1,8\}} \subset Z$, then each K is infinite and at the same time closed upon its members with $K_{ki} \not\subset K_{kj \neq i}$.

In case of random numbers let $C_r \subset \{Z\text{-}K_k\}$ and $c_i \in C_i$, then $C_i \not\subset C_j$, if $c_i > c_j$ and $C_i \subset C_j$ if $c_i < c_j$ and condition (5.14) is valid.

Thus both for K and under certain conditions C those numbers that cannot be referenced present infinite address spaces, which do not interfere with each other. These address spaces could be used to subdivide one and the same memory space in

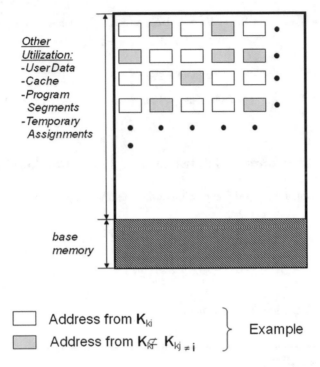

Other
Utilization:
-UserData
-Cache
-Program
_ Segments_
-Temporary
_ Assignments_

base
memory

☐ Address from K_{ki}
▨ Address from $K_{kj} \neq K_{kj \neq i}$ } Example

Fig. 5.6 Non-interfering address space

a computer for example for virtualisation purposes (Fig. 5.6). Thus memory requirements could be optimized for a given memory size.

5.6.2   Cryptography

The cryptographic transformation of symbols, for example letters, can be done via their position in the alphabet by using a key containing $\{k_i, L_i\}$ with L_i being the length of the transformation period for a particular k_i. The complete key will consist of the total sequence of variations of k_i and L_i. For encryption on the basis of random triggers the key will contain the trigger and the corresponding L or sequences thereof. Decimal numbers can be encrypted directly, if they belong to **Z**. In case of **Q** a prior multiplication by 10^m is necessary. If the resulting numbers become too large they can be presented logarithmically.

5.6.3 Computer Art

If one enters the results into Microsoft EXCEL (©) and processes these further into various types of presentations, one obtains graphs as shown in Figs. 5.7, 5.8 and 5.9: circle, net, ring. The source code for the original calculation program for the transformation can be found in the appendix to this chapter.

Alternately a presentation of 35 realisations of computer art can be found under the ISBN of this book under SpringerLink.

K=6

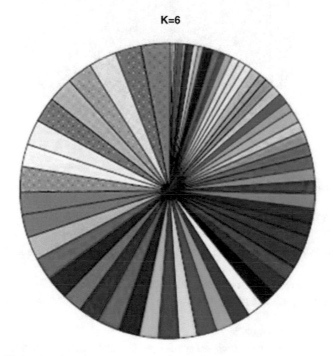

Fig. 5.7 Circle chart for k = 6

K=6

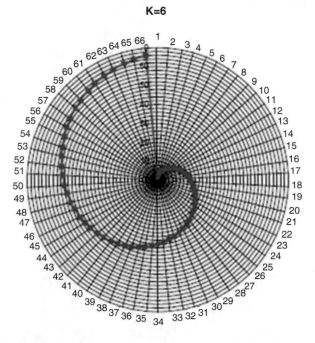

Fig. 5.8 Net chart for k = 6

5.6.4 Other

Other possible application candidates for jump transformations include:

- scalability and selection of electromagnetic impulses
- quantum physics and quantum electrodynamics; Hamiltonian as transformation sequence
- cosmology and percolation
- neurology and neurophysics, epilectology, artificial neural networks.

K=6

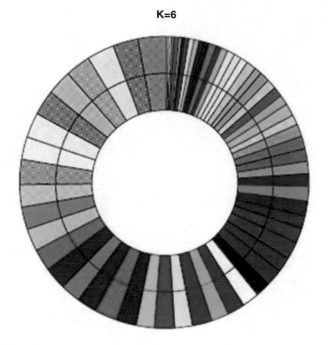

Fig. 5.9 Ring chart for $k = 6$

Appendix

Source code for computer art calculations:

```cpp
#include <fstream>
#include <iostream>
#include <iomanip>
using namespace std;
int main() {
//char adatei[10];
int k;
int a1;
int a2;
int d;
int a;
int e;
int b;
int c;
int k2;
int j;
int f;
int g;
//ofstream ausgabe;
        ofstream ausgabe("tr10.txt");
        cout << "\n Bitte den Wert von 'k' eingeben: ";
        cin >> k;
        k2=11*k;
//      cout << "Bitte Ausgabedatei eingeben: " << flush;
//      cin.getline(adatei,10,'*');
//      ausgabe.open(adatei);
        d=0;
        a=0;
        e=0;
        c=0;
        b=0;
        j=1;
        a1=0;
        a2=0;
        f=0;
            D:d=d+1;
                    a1=0;
            C:c=c+1;
//                      f=a1+a2;
            B:b=b+1;
                    a=f;
                    for (j=1; j<=k2; j++) {
                            a=a+1;
                            e=e+1;
                            ausgabe << setw(10) << a
                                    << setw(10) << e
```

```
                                             << endl;
                            cout << setw(10) << a
                                    << setw(10) << e
                                    << endl;
                    }
            f=a2+a1+b*100;
            g=f;
//          a2=a2+a;
//          a=a2;
            e=e+1;
//                                  << "e"
//                                  << cndl;
            ausgabe << setw(10) << f
                    << setw(10) << e
                    << endl;
            cout << setw(10) << f
                    << setw(10) << e
                    << endl;
                    if(b<k) {
                    goto B;
                    }
                    else {
                            a=f;
                            j=1;
                            for (j=1; j<=k2; j++) {
                                    a=a+1;
                                    e=e+1;
                                    ausgabe << setw(10) << a
                                            << setw(10) << e
                                            << endl;
                                    cout << setw(10) << a
                                        << setw(10) << e
                                        << endl;
                                            }
            a1=c*1000;
            g=a1+a2;
            e=e+1;
//          ausgabe << "a"
//                  << "e"
//                  << endl;
            ausgabe << setw(10) << g
                    << setw(10) << e
                    << endl;
            cout << setw(10) << g
                << setw(10) << e
                << endl;
```

```
                       }
                b=0;
                f=a2+c*1000;
                if(c<k) {
                goto C;
                }
                else {
                        a=g;
                        B1:b=b+1;
                                        for (j=1; j<=k2; j++) {
                                            a=a+1;
                                            e=e+1;
                                            ausgabe << setw(10) << a
                                                     << setw(10) <<e
                                                     << endl;
//                                          ausgabe << "a"
//                                                   << "e"
//                                                   << endl;
                                            cout << setw(10) << a
                                                  << setw(10) << e
                                                  << endl;
                                        }
                                        a=a1+a2+b*100;
//                              a=a1;
//                              a2=a2+a;
//                              a=a2;
                                        e=e+1;
//                                      ausgabe << "a"
//                                               << "e"
//                                               << endl;
                                        ausgabe << setw(10) << a
                                                 << setw(10) << e
                                                 << endl;
                                        cout << setw(10) << a
                                              << setw(10) << e
                                              << endl;
                                        if(b<k) {
                                        goto B1;
                                        }
                                        else {
                                        j=1;
                                        for (j=1; j<=k2; j++) {
                                        a=a+1;
                                        e=e+1;
//                                      ausgabe << "a"

//                                               << "e"
```

```cpp
//                                              << endl;
                                    ausgabe << setw(10) << a
                                            << setw(10) << e
                                            << endl;
                                        cout << setw(10) << a
                                            << setw(10) << e
                                            << endl;
                                                }
                a2=d*10000;
                }
            e=e+1;
//          ausgabe << "a"
//                      << "e"
//                      << endl;
            ausgabe << setw(10) << a2
                    << setw(10) << e
                    << endl;
            cout << setw(10) << a2
                << setw(10) << e
                << endl;
            b=0;
            c=0;
            f=a2;
                    if(d<k) {
                    goto D;
                    }
                    else {
                            a=a2;
                            a1=0;
                            C1:c=c+1;
                            B2:b=b+1;
                            for (j=1; j<=k2; j++) {
                                a=a+1;
                                e=e+1;
//                              ausgabe << "a"
//                                      << "e"
//                                      << endl;
                                ausgabe << setw(10) << a
                                        << setw(10) << e
                                        << endl;
                                    cout << setw(10) << a
                                        << setw(10) << e
                                        << endl;
                                    }
                            a=a1+a2+b*100;
//                          a1=a1+a;
```

```
//                                      a=a1;
//                                      a2=a2+a;
//                                      a=a2;
                                        e=e+1;
        //                              ausgabe << "a"
        //                                  << "e"
        //                                  << endl;
                                        ausgabe << setw(10) << a
                                                << setw(10) << e
                                                << endl;
                                        cout << setw(10) << a
                                            << setw(10) << e
                                            << endl;
                                        if(b<k) {
                                        goto B2;
                                        }
                                        else {
                                                j=1;
                                        for (j=1; j<=k2; j++) {
                                                a=a+1;
                                                e=e+1;
        //                              ausgabe << "a"
        //                                  << "e"
        //                                  << endl;
                                        ausgabe << setw(10) << a
                                                << setw(10) << e
                                                << endl;
                                        cout << setw(10) << a
                                            << setw(10) << e
                                            << endl;
                                                }
                                        a1=c*1000;
                                        g=a1+a2;
                                        e=e+1;
        //                              ausgabe << "a"
        //                                  << "e"
        //                                  << endl;
                                        ausgabe << setw(10) << g
                                                << setw(10) << e
                                                << endl;
                                        cout << setw(10) << g
                                            << setw(10) << e
                                            << endl;
                                        }
                                b=0;
                                a=g;
```

```
if(c<k) {
goto C1;
}
else {
        B3:b=b+1;
        for (j=1; j<=k2; j++) {
        a=a+1;
        e=e+1;
//      ausgabe << "a"
//              << "e"
//              << endl;
        ausgabe << setw(10) << a
                << setw(10) << e
                << endl;
        cout << setw(10) << a
             << setw(10) << e
             << endl;
        }
        a=a1+a2+b*100;
//      a1=a1+a;
//      a=a1;
//      a2=a2+a;
//      a=a2;
        e=e+1;
//      ausgabe << "a"
//              << "e"
//              << endl;
        ausgabe << setw(10) << a
                << setw(10) << e
                << endl;
        cout << setw(10) << a
             << setw(10) << e
             << endl;
        if(b<k) {
        goto B3;
        }
        else {
                j=1;
                for (j=1; j<=k2; j++) {
                a=a+1;
                e=e+1;
//      ausgabe << "a"
//              << "e"
//              << endl;
        ausgabe << setw(10) << a
                << setw(10) << e
```

```
                                                            << endl;
                                         cout << setw(10) << a
                                             << setw(10) << e
                                             << endl;
                                                 }
                            a=d*10000;
                            a2=d*10000;
                            }
                }
                a=100000;
                }
                e=e+1;
//              ausgabe << "a"
//                      << "e"
//                      << endl;
                ausgabe << setw(10) << a
                        << setw(10) << e
                        << endl;
                    cout << setw(10) << a
                        << setw(10) << e
                        << endl;
//      ausgabe.close();
        return 0;
}}
```

Reference

1. Mathematica 12.0, Wolfram Research, Inc., Champain, IL, 2019

Data Management

6

6.1 Artificial Neural Networks

6.1.1 Introduction

Artificial Neural Networks are attempts to emulate biological neural networks. These are based on the functioning and architecture of brains from living organisms—preferable humans. However, in this context one has to concede that the functioning of the human brain is understood only rudimentarily up to now.

The main building block is the artificial neuron based on the idea of a natural neuron (Fig. 6.1).

6.1.2 The Model for Artificial Neural Networks

Contrary to other AI approaches the ANN approach surpasses the purely algorithmic methods for intelligent systems. As already mentioned the functioning of the human brain is taken as a blueprint to facilitate learning capabilities and abstraction. To realize this approach completely different constructs are required than classical programming techniques. It is all about architecture.

Therefore it is necessary in the first place to understand the mechanisms of the human brain. There has been some progress but what is lacking, is an overall model explaining all facets of the human brain. We are thus still on a trail of a rough approximation to biochemistry and electrochemistry of human neural circuitry. In spite of this the results of artificial neural networks prove that science is travelling along the road to success. For some scenarios certain applications have succeeded to emulate distinct capabilities of biological neural networks.

© Springer-Verlag GmbH Germany, part of Springer Nature 2020
W. W. Osterhage, *Mathematical Theory of Advanced Computing*,
https://doi.org/10.1007/978-3-662-60359-8_6

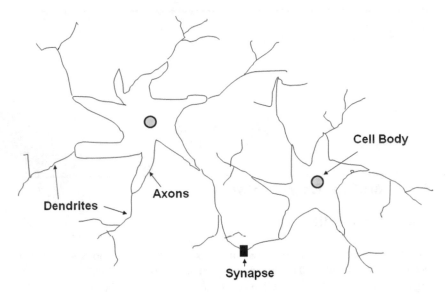

Fig. 6.1 Biological neural network

The artificial neuron had been invented to mimic the simplest characteristics of a biological neuron. To put it simply: a number of inputs act on a neuron, which are in turn outputs of other neurons. Each input has a certain weight attached to it in analogy to the strength of synaptic connections. All the weighted inputs are summarized to calculate the degree of activation of the neuron.

Although a single neuron is capable to recognize patters the strength of neural calculation is achieved through network construction. The simplest network is arranged in a single layer (Fig. 6.2). The circular nodes on the left hand side only serve to distribute the input. They have no calculation function and are thus not counted as a separate layer. They are displayed as circles to distinguish them from the calculating neurons shown as squares. Every element of the input X is connected to each artificial neuron by its own weight. Early neural networks were not more complicated than this one. Every neuron creates a weighted sum of all inputs to this network as output.

The learning effect in artificial neural networks is that it can be trained for pattern recognition for example. The learning effect is represented by the accumulation of the synaptic weight the more a connection is used—quite similar to the human brain, where quick recognition takes place, when the synaptic channels have grown stronger than other by frequent use. In a way this can be compared to the data cache of classical computers.

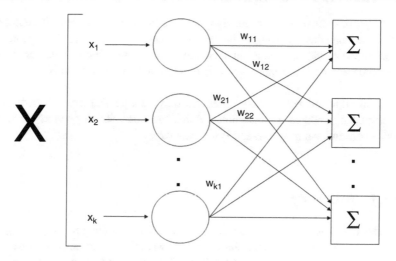

Fig. 6.2 Artificial neural network (after: Wassermann:"Neural Computing", Van Norstrand Reinhold, New York, 1989)

6.1.3   Applications

Applications for artificial neural networks are numerous. Here are some examples:

- conversion from text into spoken language
- recognition of hand written notes
- compression of images
- pattern recognition
- EEG analysis
- Radar signal processing
- market analyses
- analyses of stock exchange development

There have been proposals to employ these technologies for battle field management and babysitting. Boring, repetitive or dangerous task can be executed by these machines. The functioning of most of these networks is based on the back propagation algorithms. This algorithm proceeds in the following way:

- An input pattern is created and fed into the network.
- The output of the network is compared to a prior defined desired output. The difference between the desired and the actual output is then classified as error of the network.

- The error is then back propagated as feedback into the input layer of the network. At the same time the weights between the neuronal connections are updated in accordance with the error. In this way and through frequent iterations one approaches more and more the desired output and thus trains the network.

Artificial neural networks thus offer themselves for applications, which emulate such human intelligence transactions, which function without great effort or for which conventional programming is too expensive.

6.1.4   Reliability

Besides trivial and harmless applications such as compressing images people have thought about employing artificial neural networks in environments, which are dangerous for humans, or where the failure of these networks may lead to dangers. Therefore the question about their reliability arises.

The functioning mechanism of artificial neural networks causes that their output—similar to that of the human brain—has a certain unpredictability attached to it. The reason for this is that one does not know in detail how neuronal networks—biological or artificial—arrive at their results. The internal images in such networks are hardly retraceable. If one assumes applications, for which many such networks are interconnected with each other, a test comprising all variations to a 100% is not feasible. Therefore performance can only be estimated. This is not always acceptable. For military early warning systems this could have fatal consequences.

6.1.5   Multi-layer Neural Networks

There are two possibilities to increase the computing power of neural networks.

- Connecting many individual single layer networks
- Using multi-layer networks.

Multi-layer networks (Fig. 6.3) have capabilities surpassing those of single layer solutions. They are yet one step further in the direction to emulate the architecture of the human brain. They are constructed by superimposing single layer networks in such a way that their output serves as input to the next layer and so on.

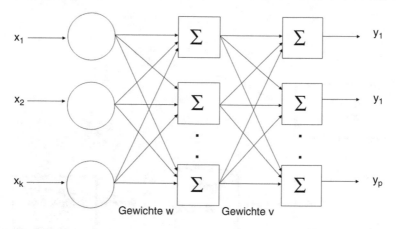

Fig. 6.3 Two layer neural network (after: Wassermann:"Neural Computing", Van Norstrand Reinhold, New York, 1989)

6.2   Data Management Concepts

Data management is a vast area and presents a high potential for application tuning. All important computers are equipped with data management features in one way or another either as part of their operating system or as separate tools with possibilities to assign logical names to files and to specify a physical storage medium. The system or the tool organises the physical space and writes data to it or reads data from it according to the user instructions in question.

The commonly used expression "data basis" in the widest sense means a collection of data records connected between each other with maximum coherence, stored in calculated redundancy and structured in such a way that different interests of many users can be satisfied (Fig. 6.4). In the following different data management systems will be touched upon. It is unavoidable that historical structures, which do not represent the state of the art of file management today, will get their mention too (Figs. 6.5 and 6.6). The reason for this is that even of today in many organisations traditional file handling is still in place, which has not been replaced by modern methods and often is a common cause for real performance problems.

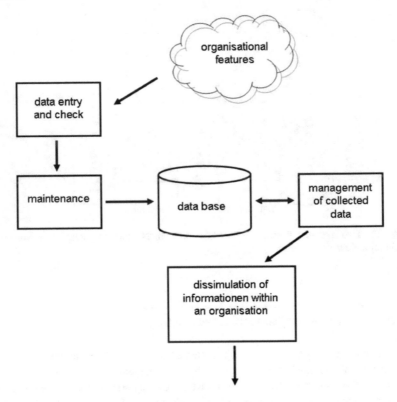

Fig. 6.4 Data basis within an organisation

| data record1 |
| data record2 |
| data record3 |
| data record4 |
| . |
| . |
| . |
| . |
| . |

Fig. 6.5 Sequential file

Fig. 6.6 Index
sequential file

index1	data record1
index2	data record2
index3	data record3
index4	data record4
	.
	.
	.
	.
	.

6.2.1   Technical Conditions

In general a data management system appears to a user as a software interface, which separates him from the operating system and at the same time from external storage hardware with respect to each access to a centrally controlled and integrated collection of data, which is shared between several applications and is called "data basis". The system provides tools to define the physical structure of the data basis and its logical connections, to load data and modify them, to protect these data against incidental damage or unauthorised access and to cater for efficient data queries. A data management system is called "generalized", if it is driven by a single user oriented command language for all these different functionalities applicable to every new data basis and independent from its internal organisation so to avoid the necessity to each time have to write new data management programs for every new data basis.

But even in such a comfortable environment there remain two unresolved problems:

- the optimisation of data mapping
- the best possible usage of advanced database management functions.

Already in 1971 standards for DBMS (Data Base Management System) were developed by the CODASYL Data Base Task Group—at that time specifically for COBOL as main host language. They proposed a network structure to model relations between data records within a common data basis (Fig. 6.7). Hierarchical relations were dealt with as being simply special cases in a chain of network files.

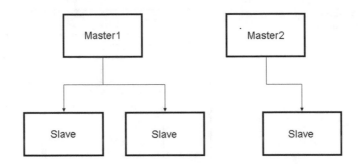

Fig. 6.7 Classical DBMS

This widely used logical structure can be found in the cross linkage of data records, which organise items within that record hierarchically or in a tree structure. In most cases most of these systems are capable of mapping a multi level hierarchy, in which sub-items may consist in turn of other sub-items and so forth.

Purely logical networks are based upon the concept of interconnected files, where each one may be allocated an owner or master record and one or more member or slave records. The higher efficiency of networks against hierarchical structures is given by the fact that one single record type may be associated with many others.

A typical DBMS comprises the following components (Fig. 6.8):

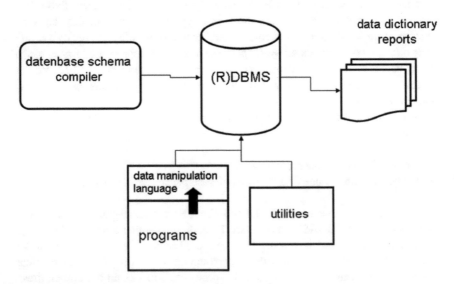

Fig. 6.8 DBMS tool box

- data description compiler
- data dictionary reports
- data manipulation language
- system modules
- utility programs.

Soon after its introduction the so called relational model exerted great influence on data management as such (Fig. 6.9). Contrary to the models discussed so far the relational model can be defined by simple rigorous mathematical concepts. Furthermore its underlying structure permits simple queries, modifications, updates and re-structuring of the database.

Altogether the relational model is more user-oriented. It views a data basis as a collection of n possible relations and homogeneous tables, in which each line corresponds to a single data record, comprising n items appearing only once. When defining relations consistency and lack of redundancy can be guaranteed once a set of formal rules is respected.

These five basic operations in relational algebra are:

- selection
- projection
- product
- aggregation and
- difference.

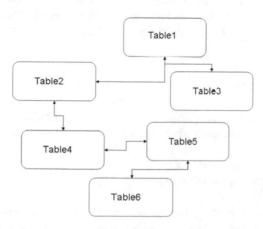

Fig. 6.9 Relational Data Base Management System (RDBMS)

reference architekture

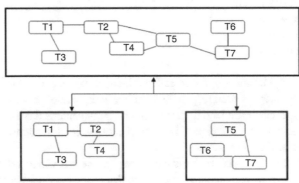

distributed databases

Fig. 6.10   Reference architecture

The next logical step in the direction of new database technologies was the development of distributed data bases. From a user point of view its principles seem relatively straight forward and transparent: applications have local characteristics on a local platform. Within a communications network data base functions coordinate access to distributed databases and pretend to a user that the data are locally available. The knowledge about the real data distribution belongs to the DBMS alone. Changes in data distribution do not entail changes in programs.

To achieve this, the DBMS relies on a so called reference architecture, comprising global and local schemata and the physical data assignment (Fig. 6.10).

6.2.2   Accesses

Independent from data management systems in operation various operating systems offer data access modalities having impact on overall performance. Those comprise:

- buffered or non-buffered access
- access with or without I/O wait.

In certain cases both options permit the continuing execution of programs without I/O processes having necessarily been completed. Besides these, table sizes as such and the overall blocking philosophy play important roles, of course. Blocking should be implemented on the lowest possible level (item), if feasible, never on table level and—if possible—also not on record level.

6.3 Knowledge Bases and Neuronal Tools

6.3.1 Introduction

Initially we shall discuss knowledge bases and their relation to AI. This will show that traditional knowledge bases arrive at their limits regarding flexibility required for AI.

This leads to options outside of knowledge bases. In sequence we shall touch upon:

- fuzzy systems
- cognitive maps
- neuronal networks.

We will explain why none of the advanced techniques alone can serve for a data base management technology surpassing today´s state of the art. As a probable consequence a Hypermodel is proposed combining different advanced as well as traditional aspects.

6.3.2 Knowledge Bases and AI

How do today´s technical solutions match the requirements regarding data management for AI systems? Or, to put it differently: how does the intelligence of DBMS fit into AI? A DBMS can be regarded as a tool within AI without acquiring the status of an independent intelligence.

On the other hand other applications outside AI cannot profit from AI experience with respect to data management technologies alone.

Why is that so? The explanation is simple: a DBMS is based on non-learning fixed rule structures and techniques while AI systems really behave flexible and should grow during knowledge acquirement—independently from the employed techniques.

To simplify this task and help for intelligence to penetrate also into DBMS one has to employ advanced technologies when further developing DBMS. The following sections will look at some of the options.

6.3.3 Advanced Options for Data Base Management

There is no single solution compensating the above mentioned deficiencies. There will also not be a general claim for a definite solution after which no new features will be necessary. In the following we shall bring together a number of technologies, which will bring us closer to our objectives than already employed technologies.

It is possible to concentrate the proposed approaches in a consolidated technological basis for hybrid data management, which can be used for future developments.

6.3.3.1 Fuzzy Techniques

Fuzzy techniques possess two advantages in comparison with classical data storage:

- non-deterministic values
- weighted information relationships.

The first point helps much more to come close to reality regarding inter-human relationships than a set of prior determined rules, from which one is allowed to select with regard to specific information requirements. Just because statements and information in everyday life are imprecise fuzzy techniques have been developed. Therefore the introduction of fuzzy attributes into a normal data basis is a step in the right direction. Furthermore the technically rigid pointers of a DBMS or the more subtle relations of an RDBMS have to be replaced by weighted connections representing fuzzy probabilities.

As a next step the concept of classical files or data sets with many data fields could be abandoned for a concept, which entwines individual data fields or data nodes.

To complete a fuzzy cognitive map positive and negative causal correlations constitute a pattern replacing a classical data management schema (Fig. 6.11).

6.3.3.2 Neural Networks

Neural networks have been introduced above. With the help of these network techniques one can design a neural data set (NDS) similar to a cognitive map as shown in Fig. 6.12.

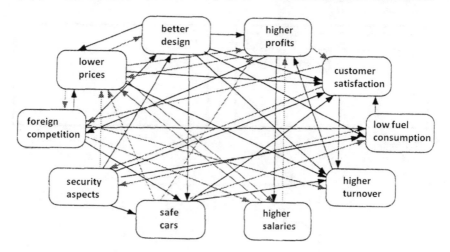

Fig. 6.11 Fuzzy cognitive map

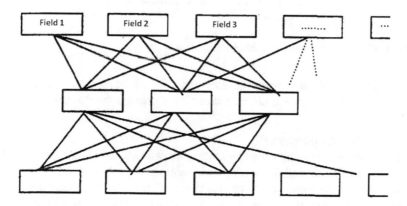

Fig. 6.12 NDS (Neural Data Set)

The functional capabilities of such data management have been demonstrated in neural network applications. But this approach alone would only result in some sort of field-related data basis. And because one generally has to deal with a large number of fields, a complete neural data basis would become unmanageable quite quickly.

One can advance the theory of such a model one more step (Fig. 6.13).

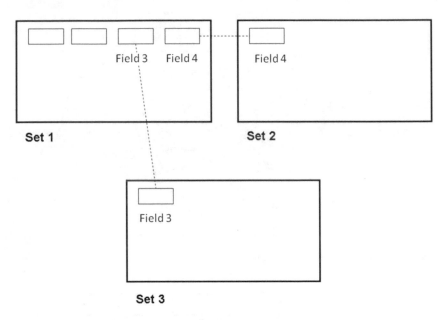

Fig. 6.13 NDBMS (Neural Data Base Management System)

In this way a three-dimensional neural structure, which combines techniques of relational data management and characteristics of neural networks, would ensue.

6.3.3.3 The Hypermodel
It is unlikely that one single basic technology known today will be the winner in the contest about a universal data management tool with regard to AI. It is much more likely that a combination of the characteristics of several proven approaches will serve as a basis to establish forward-looking developments with new ideas.

There are a number of aspects to be taken into account regarding such a hybrid model:

Elements of a hybrid model:

- data description compiler
- data dictionary reports
- data manipulation language
- fundamental operations of relational algebra
- rule bases

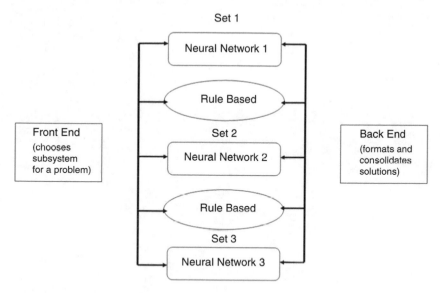

Fig. 6.14 The Hypermodel

- semantic networks
- object oriented knowledge representation
- inheritance principles
- fuzzy techniques
- cognitive maps
- neural networks.

Figure 6.14 shows an example of such a hybrid configuration.

6.3.4   Conclusion

Traditional knowledge bases with respect to their employment for AI show specific deficits. Their technologies taken one by one do not match the requirements. By taking historical as well as advanced approaches it is found that only a combination of several such techniques will result in a seminal basis: the Hypermodel. This is still a challenge for development labs: a DBMS containing among others relational, fuzzy and neural elements.

Quantum Computers

7

7.1 What Is Intelligence?

If one asks a philosopher, what intelligence is, one obtains as many answers as there are philosophers. The same result is obtained, if one puts the question to a psychologist or biologist or mathematician or information scientist. Every person has its own imagination about the subject. This is due to his own capabilities and a result of meeting with other people and all other experiences dating back to his time at school. But if we want to talk about Artificial Intelligence (AI) one has to develop some sort of target image, otherwise one may miss the objective.

What do we want to talk about, when considering intelligence in connection with AI? Do we mean that qualified intelligence playing a role when quantifying an IQ test or rather so called emotional intelligence, attributed to a person, who would not pass a traditional IQ test with good results?

Reading the pertinent literature dealing with artificial intelligence one notices immediately at what level these approaches try to grasp the subject: without intermediate steps human intelligence is taken into consideration. But this is the highest occurrence of intelligence. But not enough—apparently people are not satisfied emulating any stupid person, but of course only an "intelligent" one, i.e. a "highly intelligent" one—at the minimum in possession of the intelligence equivalent of the researcher dealing with the subject.

On the other hand there are branches of science dealing with other intelligences—for example those of apes or dogs—of course always in comparison to that of humans. However, up to now no one has achieved to emulate the intelligence of any mammal, not to mention that of a human.

There thus exists—to sum it up—biological intelligence. But this is still only natural and no artificial intelligence. Talking about artificial intelligence, it is artificial—contrary to natural—and nothing else. And this may in the end look differently and act differently as its natural model. Perhaps this would be a more modest target.

To be able to proceed we cannot do without some sort of definition.
Proposition 1:

"An intelligent system is an adaptive one."

Let us take an example from control theory or cybernetics. In Fig. 7.1 in the upper part we see a signal passing through some information route, then through a processor, getting a new value imprinted on it, leaving the processor and traveling on. This system is not intelligent, since it just takes on some information, which is imprinted on it from an external source.

A different situation arises, when the system is capable to feed back the new signal to the original input as in Fig. 7.1 below, constituting a reference value to be fed again into the processor—again and again, until a given condition is fulfilled to leave the processor with this new value. The system thus has constantly adapted itself by comparing.

Proposition 2:

"Feedback systems are adaptive and thus intelligent."

In this sense the temperature control of a radiator is an intelligent system. It measures the outside temperature, feeds this information back and in this way controls the throughput of hot water via a special mechanism.

Fig. 7.1 Signal processing

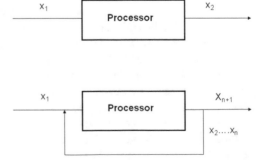

7.2   Quantum Computers

Although first considerations date back to the first half of the past century, people have only started at the beginning of the twenty-first century to implement quantum computers. Today (2019) there is a quantum processor from IBM, the "Q Experience", in operation working on the basis of 20 qubits.

A quantum computer uses the laws of quantum mechanics by processing quantum mechanical states. In this context superposition and entanglement play a role.

The fundamental quantity of a quantum computer is the qubit. Contrary to the bits in classical computers a qubit has the possibility to represent more than just one of two but by superposition many possible states. The aggregation of several qubits is called a quantum register. Qubits can be created for example by linear or circular polarized light or by spin states of electrons (up or down). Another possibility would be offered for example by the energetic states of the hydrogen atoms (ground state for a "0"; excited state for a "1"). To create these states one could use a laser beam. This would correspond to a "Write" in a classical computer. To read stored information one could again use a laser, the pulse of which would depend on the excitation state of the qubits. Elementary operations acting on a qubit are called gate.

Which are the advantages of a quantum computer against a classical system? A classical system encodes just two possible states. If we regard N systems we can implement only N codifications. The number of codifications and thus the computing capacity increase linearly. In a quantum computer the system is characterized by the ratio of the amplitudes of the occupied states: a complex number. The wave function belonging to a specific state is parameterized by N complex coefficients. Regarding the complete system of N qubits the number of simultaneously representable states increases with 2^N. This leads to an enormous computing capability.

The above considerations, however, are only applicable by phase coherence. One problem, when implementing quantum computers, is that of decoherence. Similar to the measurement problem in quantum physics the wave function collapses by loss of its coherence when interacting with the environment, i.e. with the users of quantum computers.

7.3   Implementation

There are no commercial quantum computers on the market yet (2019). IBM had presented a small demonstration unit at a computer fair. But worldwide researchers are on their way to develop quantum computer hardware in different directions. These include:

- Trapped ions, a technology related to that driving atom clocks ("Paul trap")
- Integrated circuits made of superconducting materials
- Nano structures in semiconductors
- Doped artificial diamonds
- Atoms in laser fields
- Nuclear magnetic resonance
- Photon states

One of the main problems regarding the transformation of quantum logic into hardware elements resides in its error proneness in comparison to classical digital computers. Two factors play a significant role for this:

- External influences can manipulate quantum systems.
- Decoherence

There exist theoretical models for error correction, but in practice this requires a significant overhead. In theory quantum computers should be capable to calculate anything a normal computer does, but special emphasis is on the following capabilities:

- Tap-proof messaging
- Teleportation of information
- Creation of real random numbers
- Prime factor decomposition
- Fast data bank searches
- Breaking of encryptions

Actual quantum computer systems comprise no more than 20–50 physical qubits, which is insufficient to carry out error corrected crypto analysis. To break a 2048 RSA crypto code in 1 hour about 1 billion qubits would be required. Therefore some efforts leave the main focus for quantum computing, crypto analysis, aside and concentrate on easier applications like quantum simulation.

The main constraints for a functioning quantum computer are:

- Qubits have to be well-defined and scalable
- Qubits have to be initialized under well-defined initial conditions
- A universal set of gates has to be executed coherently
- Qubits must be read in a reliable fashion.

7.4   Intelligence of Quantum Systems

Are quantum systems as such intelligent?—This brings us back to the question of the first section in this chapter: what is intelligence? We have answered that:

> "An intelligent system is an adaptive one."

and

> "Feedback systems are adaptive and thus intelligent."

A quantum system can be anything comprising one or more elementary particles interacting with each other via electromagnetism, strong or weak interaction (gravitation is left out in this context, since its role in quantum systems is at the moment subject of speculation—string theory, grand unification etc.). Particles can be described by a number of characteristics like mass, charge, spin etc. and quantum numbers.

On the other hand an intelligent system in terms of computer theory can be dissected into: processor, memory, I/O unit. If we could map these requirements onto a quantum system we could answer the above question: a particle could be designated as processor since it reacts to the information transferred by one or more of the interactions cited via the field quantum in question (Photon, Boson, Gluon). It absorbs the information and at the same time transmits information about its existence and the state it is in via the same field quantum to surrounding other particles. Thus the I/O condition is fulfilled as well. It can be excited into different states, but eventually it will decay to its original state, which it has memorized.

The answer is yes:

Quantum systems are intelligent systems.

Index

© Springer-Verlag GmbH Germany, part of Springer Nature 2020
W. W. Osterhage, *Mathematical Theory of Advanced Computing*,
https://doi.org/10.1007/978-3-662-60359-8

Printed in the United States
By Bookmasters